THE BREAD LOAF ANTHOLOGY

of Contemporary American Poetry

THE BREAD LOAF ANTHOLOGY

of Contemporary American Poetry

Edited by Robert Pack, Sydney Lea, and Jay Parini

81416

PUBLISHED FOR THE BREAD LOAF WRITERS' CONFERENCE
Middlebury College

BY UNIVERSITY PRESS OF NEW ENGLAND
Hanover and London

MIDDLEBURY COLLEGE PRESS
Published by University Press of New England, Hanover, NH 03755
© 1985 by Bread Loaf Writers' Conference/Middlebury College
All rights reserved

Printed in the United States of America 5 4 3

LIBRARY OF CONGRESS CATALOGING IN PUBLICATION DATA

Main entry under title:

The Bread Loaf anthology of contemporary American poetry.

1. American poetry—20th century. I. Pack, Robert,
1929–   . II. Lea, Sydney, 1942–   . III. Parini,
Jay. IV. Bread Loaf Writers' Conference of Middlebury College.
PS615.B65 1985   811'.54'08   85–40489
ISBN 0–87451–349–9
ISBN 0–87451–350–2 (pbk.)

FOREWORD

The poems gathered in this anthology reflect an enormous range of styles and perspectives. This book (the first in a series that will appear, we hope, every five years) represents what has happened in the past half decade of American verse.

Poetry is an essential part of any living culture; without it, a people has no passionately articulate view of itself, no voice for its aspirations or for considered self-criticism. We believe that the poems presented here demonstrate the vigor of contemporary American poetry and its ongoing controversies about the nature and use of form. American verse has survived and remained vital, for it has managed to expand and change, to age and remain young, to express both the common national experience and the diverse strains of our complex society, its many landscapes and regional concerns.

This book derives its title from the Bread Loaf Writers' Conference of Middlebury College in Vermont, which for sixty years has offered American poets a gathering place and, if not a specific credo, at least a commitment to craft and to poetry as a vehicle for exploring values: political, moral, and spiritual. Encouragement for the writing and reading of poetry at Bread Loaf continues to reaffirm the great enterprise of civilization—the consciousness of consciousness, the mind's engagement with itself through the symbolic power of language. Bread Loaf embodies a dedication to the communal sense of literature even in a country as huge as ours.

The Writers' Conference, in which many of the writers here represented have taken part, is also robust and inclusive; and—though we do not claim it as the only unifying forum for what is stimulating or triumphant in our national verse—the editors do believe that the Conference is an emblem of what makes American poetry the resource it has been, and is. These poems give evidence of concerns which hover over Bread Loaf Mountain for two weeks every August—concerns for our allegiance to values and techniques handed down by serious predecessors whose ongoing presence has been vital to every lover of the word.

The editors chose the work included here on three grounds. First, the poets themselves must have published at least two books. Our assumption is that everyone in this book has had some time to mature; his or her current poems reveal a well-developed voice. The second criterion was date of composition; all the work in this book has been written since 1980. The book thus represents a "moment" in the history of American poetry. Third, none of these poems has yet been published in individual collections. The authors have sent us their own selections from which our final selections have been made.

We offer this book as a birthday present to the Bread Loaf Writers' Conference and as a gesture of pride in a literary culture that has added immeasurably to the art of poetry in English.

ROBERT PACK
SYDNEY LEA
JAY PARINI

CONTENTS

THE BREAD LOAF ANTHOLOGY

of Contemporary American Poetry

A. R. AMMONS

Burnout in the Overshoot

The first cool spell has
cracked the white asters open,
samples here and there,

and tomorrow's promised warmth will
stir a few bees loose:
there's something besides

death and nothingness,
even if winter is coming:
and, anyway, death isn't

a place you get all the way
to: as you arrive
what is arriving

diminishes and
finally, touch to touch,
nothing is equal to nothing.

The Gathering

Where does the locus lie
or stand, high in a mind-dome
all arcs
of knowledge or perception

intersect, a dome constructed
not just of the mind's
own materials
but the world's outside,

the knowledges brought in
and flung to the mind's motions
for shaping: or isn't
the dome, if any, actually

outside, heavenward, beyond
moon haulings or
sun centerings,
a summary place so high & fine

its point of equipoise might
miss matter altogether,
lying, rising, or falling
intermediately, containing

no matter though calling it all
into alignment, and
that dome perceived, hoped or
imagined, isn't the mind's a copy,

a lessened figure, if legitimate
with accurate outline:
where is the essence of a perception
or thought, come to think of it:

and what good is a knowledge
only questions trace into defining,
the truest knowledge the richest
gathering of forming doubt:

love, the dumb & tugging yearning,
undermines us into
simpler motions, the lure a single
place and that place

circulating throughout us:
is the dome, the arc-nexus,
something love fashioned,
the sweetest burden

to impose on the galaxies: maybe, for
inwardly the libido issues from
summary extensions, flows through
our wishes, minds without obstruction

(or bleakly with), goes outside
and includes what is and builds
it up, so that the dome stands
radiant as an eye,

transfixing as the majesty of
a nipple not yet touched:
or does love go just so far,
its net gathering the couplings,

families, friends, peoples
but then transfering its force
to the severe redemptions of
harsh necessity: when we lie

dying, what are we to think:
of the light that would seem
to have no undoing in the head
even though commonly the

head rots off: or are we to think
on the unending brilliance
way overhead that doesn't quail to
darkness, but may never have

known it produces us or lets
us go: how could we have been
produced except by knowing means:
there in the center the face

we've found freedom to impose
without imposition invites us to
come along, saying yes to losses:
beyond the sun, the mind's sun shines.

JOHN ASHBERY

Endless Variation

At some point in the pageant there is a moment
Of complete quiet. That is when you grab the urchin
By the hair and hold his head firmly
In the rush of water from the hydrant
As he metamorphoses by turns into a frog,
An ostrich, a rhinoceros, an electric eel,
And further things too solemn to identify, as though
They had waited for the others to give up before
Asserting a definitive muteness. And as there is no longer
Anything to interpret, you must now return

To the debate, the quarrel of the ancients and moderns,
That flutes more shrilly as each succeeding century
Resumes it. What must happen on the stage?
And in whose interest is it all, finally?
It is wise to pay attention so that the final plea
Of the defense will mean something, before the case is rested,
Though we know it will end in a tie again.
Yet the result is always the product of an elsewhere
Beyond these sounds, these signs that build an argument
That falls short, every time. It would be the same
If no one had left home, except for the tingle
Of frost in the air, overruled, expectant, that means us well.

By the Flooded Canal

Which custard? The dish of not-so-clean snow
Or the sherry trifle with bloodlike jam and riotous
Yellow stuff running down the steep sides
Into ambiguity, an ambiguous thing. Do you want me
To come here anymore.

Then I met your father.
I hadn't written anything for almost a year.

Unfortunately he wasn't very attractive.

He married a woman with the curious name of Lael.
It all took me by surprise, coming up behind me
Like a book. As I stand and look at it now.
Then all the thoughts went out of my head,
Running away into the wind. I didn't have *him*
To think about anymore, I didn't have myself either.
It was all notes for a book, or footnotes, footnotes
For a book that has been written, that nobody
Is ever going to read. A bottle with a note in it
Washes up on shore and no one sees it, no one picks it up.

And then one day it was windy
With fog, and I hate the combination of fog and wind,
Besides being too cool for what it looked like. The sun
Was probably out just a short distance above our heads.
Not a good drying day. And I hung the laundry out
On the clothesline, all black and white
And the news got lost somewhere inside. My news.

Do you come here any longer with the intention of killing
Something, no you have nothing in mind.
And I shift, arranging the pieces
In a cardboard drawer. No two are alike, and I like that.

The kitten on the stairs heard it
Once, in disbelief, and I go
To sales, and buy only what we need.
The old men are a strong team.

And I mix it up with them, it's quite like
Having encounters if one is a poplar
In a row of them and so involved
With one's reflection as well as one's two neighbors only I say
I didn't mean for it to be this way
But since it has happened I'm glad and will continue to work,
To strive for your success. I don't expect thanks
And am happy in the small role assigned me,
Really. I think I'll go out in the garage.

Nothing to Steal

What's growing? Will it start
In the next few minutes, leaving us
Far from each other? I think he said
The sun is going down in Florida, but the proverb
Tells us there is no night in light,
No respite, no ticking in the separate seconds.
The prospect is such verbiage, a winter
Landscape, dense, tangled.

A loner spied it in his vocabulary
And, about to shy, made the rest
Into man instead. Dread is the pillow
Of those who flee, making more in the morning.
By midafternoon the machine
Has gasped its last. There are no things to be,
Only a detective. A light dusting of snow
Was all he was appalled to find. On the tree

A mile away some dim, swollen, waxen fruit. He couldn't
Go on
Enumerating. They came for the sale,
Students weighing protests, a light on
In the garage. Those in the superette
Shirked their idea more hazily. The sun
Had now returned to the kitchenette.

Bite harder, the old man tells them, the next time
The rabbit wars loom and you got all scratched
In the basin. Next time. And wear wool
Headgear 'cause the car's scrapped, the children
Came out to see what was wrong and we all turned
In that direction, only to have it disappear.
There are parking lights shining and who knows
How much of it they take in let alone
Understand though the stairs are nice
And the companions in the yards too who fall
In all directions. Standing's the comparison
For them as don't want to sleep yet after
All, after it was all over, one sees some
Disappointment in breaths sucked in, in
The decision to wait until the same time tomorrow
For the wolf to be on, whose hunger
Made him leave the woods, and the sea
Must be part of that too. The wire sea.

Wet Are the Boards

Not liking what life has in it,
"It's probably dead, whatever it is,"
You said, and turned, and thought
Of one spot on the ground, what it means to all of us
Passing through the earth. And the filleted, reasonable
Nymph of the fashions of the air points to that too:
"No need to be deprived. We are all
Friends here,
And whatever it takes to get us out of the mess we're in,
One of us has."

Charming, you thought. The spirited bulk,
The work of a local architect, knows how to detach itself
From the little puffs issuing from the mouths of the four winds,
Yet not too much, and be honest
While still remaining noble and sedate.
The tepees on the front lawn
Of the governor's palace became a fixture there
And were cast in stone when the originals rotted away.
Fish tanks glinted from within the varnished
Halls of jurisprudence and it was possible to save
The friezes, of Merovingian thrust,
And so much else made to please the senses
Like a plum tree dripping besmirched brilliants
On a round dirt bed, and all the stories of the ducks.
Now if only I were a noncombatant—
Which brings us back to the others: philosophers,
Pedants, and criminals intent on enjoying the public view—
Is it just another panorama

In my collection, or do I belong to it
As long as it wishes to regard me? For we none of us
Can determine strictly what they are thinking,

Even the one we walk arm in arm with
Through the darkling purple air of spring, so when it comes
Time to depart our goodbyes will read automatically true or false
According to what has gone before.
And that loneliness will accompany us
On the far side of parting, when what we dream, we read.
No hand is outstretched
Through the bored gloom unless more thinking wants to take us
    elsewhere
Into a space that seems changed, by luck or just by time hanging around,
And the mystery of the family that bore you
Into the race that is.

And get involved in it we did, reversing the story
So that the end showed through the paper as the beginning
And all children were nice again.
Think again of the scenery
Whirling to destroy itself, and what a different face
It wears when order smiles, as I know it
Does here. The costumes we wore
Must never be folded and put back into the trunk again,
Or someone too young for the part is going to step up
And say, "Listen, I made it. It's mine,"
In a November twilight when the frost is creeping over you
As surely as waves across a beach, since no chill is complete
Without your unique participation. And when you walk away
You might reflect that this is an aspect
In which all of the cores and seeds are visible.
It's a matter of not choosing to see.

MARVIN BELL

Long Island

The things I did, I did because of trees,
wildflowers and weeds, because of ocean and sand,
because the dunes move about under houses built on stilts,
and the wet fish slip between your hands back into the sea,
because during the War we heard strafing across the Bay
and after the War we found shell casings with our feet.
Because old tires ringed the boat docks,
and sandbags hung from the prows of speedboats,
and every road in every country ends at the water,
and because a child thinks each room in his house big,
and if the truth be admitted, his first art galleries
were the wallpaper in his bedroom and the carlights
warming the night air as he lay in bed counting.

The things I did, I counted in wattage and ohms,
in the twelve zones that go from pure black to pure white,
in the length of the trumpet and the curves of the cornet,
in the cup of the mouthpiece. In the compass and protractor,
in the perfect bevelled ruler, in abstract geometry,
and if the truth be known, in the bowing of cattails
he first read his Heraclitus and in the stretching box turtle
he found his theory of relativity and the gist of knowledge.
He did what he did. The action of his knee in walking
was not different from the over-stretching of an ocean wave,
and the proofs of triangles, cones and parallelograms
were neither more nor less than the beauty of a fast horse
which runs through the numbers of the stopwatch and past the finish.

The things I counted, I counted beyond the finish,
beyond rolling tar roadways that squared the fields,
where I spun on the ice, wavered in fog, sped up or idled,
and, like Perry, like Marco Polo, a young man I saw
alone walk unlit paths, encircled by rushes
and angry dogs, to the indentations of his island.
And if the truth be told, he learned of Columbus,
of Einstein, of Michelangelo, on such low roads and local waters.
Weakfish hauled weakening from the waters at night,
and the crab rowing into the light, told him in their way
that the earth moved around the sun in the same way,
with the branched mud-print of a duck's foot to read,
and life in the upturned bellies of the fishkill in the creek.

Tideline

There I buried the wishfulness and the watchfulness that was in me,
by the tideline of the Atlantic,
under the stars which had come up onto the beach in families:
constellations of fish the size of a fingertip,
stars lost among the shark's egg pouch
and the tiny drums of bone swept from the spines
of the sea's plenty. No man has given more than I
to the ocean, for I took the felt word of it
with me into the middle of this country's basin,
and with it I kept the ground breathing its way,
and the flowers that grow at the tip ends of weeds
grew higher weaving in the breezes to spot water.

It isn't death to feed a white gull from miles away in the dirt,
though death is in the water and the dirt,
and it isn't death to squint into the spray by the shoreline,
though the wind throws back in your face

the burly call of the painterly fishermen
whom the fog scales of imperfections.
                              This life isn't the last word
but the born among us moving ever farther inland
with damp trouser cuffs and sand in our shoes
to where the tropical sea life has turned into gravel,
and I myself can pick up the Ice Age
in fossils and topsoil. Isn't this it?
Sometimes in the dunes, I wanted to stop breathing.

Song for a Little Bit of Breath

To Dorothy

I still have this vertical pain under my left shoulder blade.
Sometimes in the morning, the roadway by the front door
has this slick layer of new rain over it,
and the ground gets frost, and the grass its white hair.
I've got this finger tip of open space on my scalp
that once took stitches, and a slice through my right eyebrow
that took stitches, and a streak remains on my forehead
where recently we were together when the door hit me.

Some of our quietest moments lay either side of thunder.
Around us, lightning lit all—we were there to see it.
Our back porch stretched out into the middle of shooting stars,
and we felt a little bit of breath go out on each trail.
I still have this pain that falls through the entire night sky
in my shoulder, where, when the thunder has stopped,
your head has lain on my arm for twenty-five years.
I am taking bolts of lightning to cure it, and the space
around the thunder is a cure. But I wish on every star,
falling or not, that it isn't taken from me here.

Quilt, Dutch China Plate

This was sanity—of star and snowflake,
grateful for scraps and thread and bits of dust
from under the bed. Thank you for needles.
This was the prairie place the wind could not pass through
looking for a lap, the compass that pointed to home.
Here are the points within a circle, the circle
defined by its points, the articulations of fingers.
And here, wordless, are the stops between the points,
the circles inside a ring, and the copycat's square.
Here is the pinwheel, the medicine wheel, the coin as art.
Here is the wagon wheel, the train, the miles, the Midwest.
The sun is here, spinning. The eye, too, is set spinning.
These are the propellors, the fans, the slight twisting on its axis
of the pie and the plate and the bucket
whenever one was set down for a moment. This is time frozen
and the work of women. Here is how long
the absolute *now* is, the dilemma of steadfastness,
not pretty. The invisible repeats itself—
manifest sunflowers, the moon in the water.
What is to be done with such an object,
which says beautifully that design is the motion a shape makes?
—while petals bloom in the brain, and the blood
bursts to break things high overhead.

A Path among the Dunes

Long waves of form, and what if under a sandhill
Socrates finds a bird? If Plato finds a lobster claw?
If down the beach someone walks precisely in my footsteps,
noticing, noting, taking pictures of my confusion,
writing down that, at this time of the morning,
the wheel tracks of the sand cabs approach
the color-gathering property of furrows in a plowed field.
Will there be time to try to fix the dunes in mind?

The light on the sand is airless and flat,
and the sand is as white as the sun itself in Space—
our steps crunch into the round grains.
At the shoreline, white light twists the juice
from the waves, and white light rakes the beach of color.

It is pure *Portrait of the Artist*, the living
among the lifeless, and the distance between them in the mind.
In the mind, the wind uses a bird to express itself.

And the sand—the sand is a flatbed of desire and remains.

WENDELL BERRY

From *Sabbaths*

I

Another Sunday morning comes
And I resume the standing Sabbath
Of the woods, where the finest blooms
Of time return, and where no path

Is worn but wears its makers out
At last, and disappears in leaves
Of fallen seasons. The tracked rut
Fills and levels; here nothing grieves

In the risen season. Past life
Lives in the living. Resurrection
Is in the way each maple leaf
Commemorates its kind, by connection

Outreaching understanding. What rises
Rises into comprehension
And beyond. Even falling raises
In praise of light. What is begun

Is unfinished. And so the mind
That comes to rest among the bluebells
Comes to rest in motion, refined
By alteration. The bud swells

Opens, makes seed, falls, is well,
Being becoming what it is:
Miracle and parable
Exceeding thought, because it is

Immeasurable; the understander
Encloses understanding, thus
Darkens the light. We can stand under
No beam that is not dimmed by us.

The mind that comes to rest is tended
In ways that it cannot intend;
Is borne, preserved, and comprehended
By what it cannot comprehend.

Your Sabbath, Lord, thus keeps us by
Your will, not ours. And it is fit
Our only choice should be to die
Into that rest, or out of it.

III

To sit and look at light-filled leaves
May let us see, or seem to see,
Far backward as through clearer eyes
To what unsighted hope believes:
The blessed conviviality
That sang Creation's seventh sunrise,

Time when the Maker's radiant sight
Made radiant every thing He saw,
And every thing He saw was filled
With perfect joy and life and light.
His perfect pleasure was sole law;
No pleasure had become self-willed.

For all His creatures were His pleasures
And their whole pleasure was to be
What He made them; they sought no gain
Or growth beyond their proper measures,
Nor longed for change or novelty.
The only new thing could be pain.

MICHAEL BLUMENTHAL

Dusk: Mallards on the Charles River

So much like an old couple on their nightly walk
that they must, in fact, be one, they come now,

webbing their way shoreward in the late light,
against the burnt sienna of the fading boathouses,

as in the dream of tranquility we all dream,
as if akin to the small solace that words bring

to a man sitting alone, at dusk, on a park bench.
And they are wishless against the soft ripplings

of the passing boats, they simply are what they are
(hardly sexed in the afterglow of the back-lit sky,

tandemed to strokes that must have preceded desire).
It is their lacks that we envy them for: speech,

torpor, boredom and blind lust. It is the silence
of their passing this warm night that brings us

again to what we might have become in this life
if not human—this and the doused sun dipping now

like a bronzed wafer into the communion of evening.
And the bass urging their circles of water outward

toward the petulant lovers. And the darkening walls:
night-struck and covered with ivy all in vain.

What a Time!

To dance, at a dark party, to old tunes
is not really to move: It's like chatter
at a long table, all in vain, and the moon
rising elsewhere. But it shakes up the bladder,

yes it does, and though your lovely partner
may indeed be your wife, wouldn't it be nice,
you say to yourself, to dance with his, smarter
maybe than yours is, but not as lovely: no sunrise

in *her* eyes to be sure. And look how easily
lust glides through these rooms, the discs
still turning with their dark, oiled and breezy
calm against the turntable. No one here risks

anything if they'll just leave early, keep
their eyes on their spouses, and moderate
their drinking. Soon they will all be asleep.
In fact, already he's whispering: "Dear, it's late,"

which means, in French: *Quelle tristesse*
habite les heures du soir! Quel dommage!
And yet you know the truth: You're blessed
to be here, in this dark, converted garage,

wasting the evening in such syncopated style,
dancing to music you never liked, even then,
kissing the nape of your wife's neck, all the while
dreaming of his, remembering how it was when

you were young, flamboyant, brazenly single
among the carefully arranged candles
and the doctored punch. How you could mingle
then! But now, you'd like to have a handle

on your passions, or so you think. In your maturity,
you're nice to everyone, hardly ever sexual, and
evenings, alone with friends, discuss the purity
of marriage. Would, now, you weren't so textual

in your resolve: You could move quietly, to Martha
and the Vandellas, into the dark, adjacent room
with your friend's wife, remembering your father
who, quoting Nietzsche about women and doom,

said: *Carry a large stick.* You're the new norm now,
though: detailed and calm, all high monogamous.
You know desire, in the end, is hardly ever amorous.
Yeah man, and off you bop into the night, transformed.

The Tip of the Iceberg

Say language really does
what it says it does:

That the bird in your hand
is really a bird, that it takes two
to tango, that whoever digs
his own grave will have to sleep in it.
Say you have a fool for a friend,
feckless and dissipated and greedy
beneath the stars, and that it takes one
to know one. Say that might
makes right, that the best offense
is a good defense, that fools rush in
while trepid angels stammer
in front of the doormats. Say
that life's unfair, that that's
the way it is, that someone tells you

"have a nice day" and really means it.
What would it be like: the word,
reticent and calm, urged out
once again toward its true meaning—
"the worst" really the worst,
"the best" the best, the sum of all
your "everythings" really, now,
everything, even the blurbs
on the back of your own books
as true as their good intentions?
What would it mean if "until death
do us part" really meant *until all breath
leaves me, love*, if "forever" meant
until the tides cease? What would signify
if "love" could only mean *love* once again,
not just the tip of the iceberg, sinking,
and in all sincerity.

PHILIP BOOTH

After the Rebuilding

After the rebuilding was done, and
the woodstove finally installed, after
the ripping-out of walls, tearing back to
its beams the house he'd lived in, frozen, for over
fifty years, he started mornings up with the world's
most expensive kindling. Not just scraps of red oak from
new flooring, ends of clear birch from kitchen trim, and
knots from #2 pine, but oddlot pieces of his old life:
window frames clawed from his daughter's lost room,
his grandfather's coat peg, shelving his mother
had rolled her crust on, and lathing first plastered
the year Thoreau moved to Walden. The woodstove itself
was new: the prime heat for four new rooms descended
from seven, the central logic for all the opening up,
for revisions hammered out daily, weeks of roughing-in,
and after months of unfigured costs, the final bevels
and the long returning. Oh, when he first got up to
rekindle the fire of November mornings, he found
that everything held heat: he sweat as he tossed
the chunks in; he found himself burning, burning.

Where Tide

The afternoon almost gone. The tide
at a certain stage of its changing.
The shore giving way to the tide,

the day giving way toward week's end.
Between us and the sea: an inlet
too small to wade, a clump of marshgrass,

a sandspit about to be flooded.
Behind us, a steep summer field.
Our backs braced against riprap,

we sat facing the tide, the tide
of the light as it capped small waves
and angled into our faces, deepening

as the tide flooded and the light ebbed.
All this was certain. The planet,
not an infinite place, kept

turning on its accustomed axis. We
were another matter, not altogether
apart, but having to face,

in each other's face, how we had
in ourselves faced change. Who,
beyond us, could say what happened;

what part of ourselves could we tell?
We were tidal; where tide measured,
we watched light dull and fog come.

A loon called out of the fog. We heard
another. Of ourselves we could make
no song. We only knew, beyond us,

how light came over the spit,
how fog came over the light, and
how the inlet broadened. After

we'd said as much as we could,
we waded up into the dark
of the still steep field behind us.

Procession

A white-throat flicked into the sunset window.
How small a thing to bury: his short neck limp,
eye perfectly blank, the feathers warm in my hand.

Nothing left now to whistle *Old Sam Peabody*,
Peabody, Peabody . . . The rest in their thickets,
knowing to go. The winter stars coming. Out early

this morning I see Orion, the first time this fall,
Aldebaran brilliant in Taurus, the Dipper's
handle tipped down toward daybreak. As sun-up

dims Venus, I walk the first frost out into ground fog,
as it happens. Slowly, it comes to me: today
would be father's 85th birthday. I hear

today's birds in the cedars, woken, knowing to go.
I think of a boy years beyond me, back in Council Bluffs,
a boy with father's name, out on a third-floor porch

after midnight, without knowing why, watching (he must
have told me hundreds of times) against his own horizon
these same winter stars beginning to show.

North Haven

Two old friends, dead too early.
September. and then May. Now
here, July, high mid-
                    July: the lettuce
tidal with dew, the hedge grown tall
with cedar waxwings. A ruby-throat holds
in mid-air,
                    sipping long at the feeder.
Given death, our fortune is to
live the life the dead left without words,
to take as given that the boats are in,
the first crop hay.
                    High season
is where we've arrived: bright
as white paint on white clapboard,
the sun becomes our custom:
                    clean of dreams,
we climb out of sleep into weather:
eased from fog, we take ourselves
for a morning dip. And stay
and stay to swim:
                    every day
we stay we keep on arriving: here
or nowhere, tide on tide, we have time
to accept:
                    we have the weather,
we have our lives: to days
like these we have ourselves to give.

DAVID BOTTOMS

Ice

No one this far south chances ice.
So what was I to think when I sat down for breakfast
on the morning after Christmas
and saw through our glazed kitchen window
the whole pond frozen white,
and out of the stiff green pines on the far side
of the pond, our neighbor's teenage daughter
edging down the bank
one careful step at a time, a boot on a rock,
a boot on a ledge? She stopped at the lip of the ice,
picked up a rock as large as a brick
and threw it out, watched it chip the surface
and slide. Then holding to a pine branch,
put one foot out and tried her weight.
I ran slow as a glacier,
or seemed to, as I pushed from the table,
and when she let go and shuffled away
from the bank, what could I do
but stand on my deck and shout the warning
that froze in the breath between us?
In the middle of the pond, all around her water
turned into something strange,
she began, of all things,
to shift on one leg, then the other,
each step sure as a prophecy,
each foot kicking thunder into the heads
of fish. Then up on her toes,
one leg sweeping her into a spin, arms flung out,

mittens like a blue dream circling her head.
And when she heard me and spun to a dizzy stop,
saw me in my ragged underwear,
barefoot on my deck,
when her hands came down to lift the hem
of an imaginary skirt
and she curtsied and turned and walked away,
I remembered a story her father told of growing up
poor in small town Ohio,
how every year in the hard of winter
the mayor drove a rattletrap onto the river
and the lottery began.

Naval Photograph: 25 October 1942: What the Hand May Be Saying

Reports of a Japanese surface presence have brought them speeding
into Savo Sound,
false reports that will not be true for days.

So now at evening the fleet drops anchor, the crews relax,
the heat drifts west toward the war in Africa.

On the deck of the tender *Tangier*
a sailor focuses a camera on a foreground of water,
the cruiser *Atlanta*, and far back against the jungles of Savo
the hulks of Task Group 66.4.

A few on the cruiser notice him, but you cannot tell it
from their faces, too many shadows, too long a stretch
of grainy water. Still,
figures can be seen loafing on the bow, leaning
from the bridge, the machine gun platforms, even a sailor
clowning on a gun turret, barrel straight up between his legs.

And behind the shadow draped like armor across that stern,
my father is standing with the gunners
under turret number six, a shadow
in a wide cluster of shadows waving toward the *Tangier*.

Knowing their future, I imagine
some pulse in the nerves, primitive as radar, throbbing,

and exactly what the hand is saying, even he does not know.
He is only standing where the living and the dead
lean against the rail,
unsure who is who, and wave across the sound
toward the camera, toward us, for all of the reasons anyone waves.

The Desk

Under the fire escape, crouched, one knee in cinders,
I pulled the ball-peen hammer from my belt,
cracked a square of window pane,
the gummed latch, and swung the window,
crawled through that stone hole into the boiler room
of Canton Elementary School, once Canton High,
where my father served three extra years
as star halfback and sprinter.
                    Behind a flashlight's
cane of light, I climbed a staircase almost a ladder
and found a door. On the second nudge of my shoulder,
it broke into a hallway dark as history,
at whose end lay the classroom I had studied
over and over in the deep obsession of memory.

I swept that room with my light—an empty blackboard,
a metal table, a half-globe lying on the floor
like a punctured basketball—then followed

that beam across the rows of desks,
the various catalogs of lovers, the lists
of all those who would and would not do what,
until it stopped on the corner desk of the back row,
and I saw again, after many years, the name
of my father, my name, carved deep into the oak top.

To gauge the depth I ran my finger across that scar,
and wondered at the dreams he must have lived
as his eyes ran back and forth
from the cinder yard below the window
to the empty practice field
to the blade of his pocket knife etching carefully
the long angular lines of his name,
the dreams he must have laid out one behind another
like yard lines, in the dull pre-practice afternoons
of geography and civics, before he ever dreamed
of Savo Sound or Guadalcanal.
                                    In honor of dreams
I sank to my knees on the smooth oiled floor,
and stood my flashlight on its end.
Half the yellow circle lit the underedge of the desk,
the other threw a half-moon on the ceiling,
and in that split light I tapped the hammer
easy up the overhang of the desk top. Nothing gave
but the walls' sharp echo, so I swung again,
and again harder, and harder still in half anger
rising to anger at the stubborn joint, losing all fear
of my first crime against the city, the county,
the state, whatever government claimed dominion,
until I had hammered up in the ringing dark
a salvo of crossfire, and on a frantic recoil glanced
the flashlight, the classroom spinning black
as a coma.
                    I've often pictured the face of the teacher

whose student first pointed to that topless desk,
the shock of a slow hand rising from the back row,
their eyes meeting over the question of absence.
I've wondered too if some low authority of the system
discovered that shattered window,
and finding no typewriters, no business machines,
no audio-visual gear missing, failed to account for it,
so let it pass as minor vandalism.
                                    I've heard nothing.
And rarely do I fret when I see that oak scar leaning
against my basement wall, though I wonder what it means
to own my father's name.

HAYDEN CARRUTH

No Matter What, after All, and That Beautiful Word So

This was the time of their heaviest migration,
And the wild geese for hours sounded their song
In the night over Syracuse, near and far,
As they circled toward Beaver Lake up beyond
Baldwinsville. We heard them while we lay in bed
Making love and talking, and often we lay still
Just to listen. "What is it about that sound?"
You said, and because I was in my customary
Umbrage with reality I answered, "Everything
Uncivilized," but knew right away I was wrong.
I examined my mind. In spite of our loving
I felt the pressure of the house enclosing me,
And the pressure of the neighboring houses
That seemed to move against me in the darkness,
And the pressure of the whole city, and then
The whole continent, which I saw
As the wild geese must see it, a system
Of colored lights creeping everywhere in the night.
Yes, the McDonald's on the strip outside Casper,
Wyoming (which I could only indistinctly remember),
Was pressing against me. "Why permit it?"
I asked myself. "It's a dreadful civilization,
Of course, but the pressure is yours." It was true.
I listened to the sound in the sky, and I had no
Argument against myself. The sound was unlike
Any other, indefinable, unnameable—certainly
Not a song, as I had called it. A kind of discourse,
The ornithologists say, in a language unknown

To us; a complex discourse about something
Altogether mysterious. Yet so is the cricketing
Of the crickets in the grass, and it is not the same.
In the caves of Lascaux, I've heard, the Aurignacian
Men and women took leave of the other animals, a trauma
They tried to lessen by painting the animal spirits
Upon the stone. And the geese are above our window.
Oh, what is it about that sound? Talking in the sky,
Bell-like words, but only remotely bell-like,
A language of many and strange tones above us
In the night at the change of seasons, talking unseen,
An expressiveness—is that it? Expressiveness
Intact and with no meaning? Yet we respond,
Our minds make an answering, though we cannot
Articulate it. How great the unintelligible
Meaning! Our lost souls flying over. The talk
Of the wild geese in the sky. It is there. It is so.

"Sure," Said Benny Goodman,

"We rode out the depression on technique." How gratifying and how
    rare,
Such expressions of a proper modesty. Notice it was not said
By T. Dorsey, who could not play a respectable "Aunt Hagar's" on a
    kazoo,
But by the man who turned the first jazz concert at Carnegie Hall
Into an artistic event and put black musicians on the stand with
    white ones equally,
The man who called himself Barefoot Jackson, or some such,
In order to be a sideman with Mel Powell on a small label
And made good music on "Blue Skies," etc. He knew exactly who he
    was, no more, no less.
It was rare and gratifying, as I've said. Do you remember the
    Incan priestling, Xtlgg, who said,

"O Lord Sun, we are probably not good enough to exalt thee," and got himself
Flung over the wall at Macchu Picchu for his candor?
I honor him for that, but I like him because his statement implies
That if he had foreseen the outcome he might not have said it.
But he did say it. *Candor seeks its own unforeseeable occasions.*
Once in America in a dark time the existentialist flatfoot floogie stomped across the land
Accompanied by a small floy floy. I think we shall not see their like in our people's art again.

Language As Inevitable Metaphor. Idea As Inevitable Figment

. . . for we all of us, grave or light, get our thoughts entangled in metaphors, and act fatally on the strength of them.
—GEORGE ELIOT

I mind once on a forenoon in early summer sitting
On his side-steps with old Steve Washer that was, reading
The paper and talking about the craziness of that year's
Election campaigns, the way people do, though it was long ago
When I was a young fellow about 45, and I don't remember
Who were the elephants and the jackasses, or which we most disfavored,
Or whether we gave it much of a nevermind, but after a while
The topic wore out, don't you know, and we sat silent together
Looking out toward the barn or across the road to the orchard
And the day pasture which were a smitch hazy in the warm sun,
And then I said, sort of half afraid—because that was
Vermont, of course, and folk there don't concert overmuch
With sentiment, though happen once in a swath of days they do,
And then it's twice as commodious, if you see my meaning—
I said, "Mr. Washer, you have a mighty good-looking farm," to which
He made no answer for a time, squinting out at the ancient ellum

That rose and descended again on the knob of the pasture,
And then he said, "I guess. I guess you might say for now
It's in a pretty good state of cultivation."
                                        I guess I might have.
Tidy it was, with all those smooth green knolls and swales
And the trees and all, but I recollect the colors most, I think,
All spring and summer, dandelions and bluets, mustard and vetch,
The buttercups that cows won't eat, and daisies and hawkweed
And black-eyed susans and joe pye weed and goldenrod, so many
Wonderful weeds, the meadow rue and salsifee—I don't rightly
Conceive how many any more—the weeds, we called them, though
We meant something a shade different in the word and we let
Them grow, thistle and yarrow and all. Not like here.
Look, the little lawns, the hedges, those foreign-appearing
Trees, but the lawns mostly, squared off and snubbed tight, grass
So bright it looks prefabricated, pre-*cultivated*, or like green
Plastic it might be, with nary weeds. Why, they even do off
The violets. I believe there's a thing like over-tidiness, or call it
Over-cultivation, that's more the nub, old proven ways grown
Lopsidal and disproportionate, cultivation for no purpose
And too refined, and the weeds poisoned. Who could have reckoned
People would put poison on the land? Of course I'm nothing,
An old man stopping here a spell before he goes his journey.
Like as not I'm misremembering. But it seems as though
I most could see those colors still and smell the sweetness
On the air at sunset, when the swallows glean the sky.

A Post-Impressionist Susurration for the First of November, 1983

Does anything get more tangled and higgeldy-piggeldy than the days as
  they drop all jumbled and
One by one on the historical heap? Not likely. And so we are all, in
  spite of ourselves, jackstraw diarists.
This afternoon Cindy and I went walking on the towpath of the Erie
  Canal, which was strangely
Straight and narrow for our devious New England feet. Yet it was
  beautiful, a long earthen avenue
Reaching far ahead of us into the shifting gossamer veils that hung
  everywhere in folds, oaks clinging to their dark leaves,
Bare maples in their many shades of gray, the field of goldenrod gone
  to seed and burnt-out asters,
Sumac with dark cones, the brown grasses, and at the far edge, away
  from the canal,
A line of trees above which towered three white pines in their singular
  shapes.
I have never seen a white pine growing naturally that was not unique
  and sculpturesque.
Why should one not devote one's life to photographing white pines, as
  Bentley of Jericho
Spent his photographing snowflakes? But it's too late, of course. At
  all events the colors,
Nor forgetting cattails and milkweed, dock and sorbaria, ferns and
  willows and barberries,
Were a nearly infinite variety of the soft tones, the subtle tones,
  made even more indistinct
In their reflections on the greenish water of the canal. And a light
  breeze was blowing.
For once I will risk the word *zephyr*, which is right and which reminds
  me of *sapphire*,
And I realize that beneath all these colors lay an undertone of blue,
  the gentle sky as it curls

Below the penumbra of vision. A small yellow butterfly tricked its way
  across the brown field beside us,
And I thought to myself, Where in hell did you come from? Last night
  was a hard frost.
And then I knew it had been born this day, perhaps a moment ago, and
  its life was flickering, flickering out in our presence
As we walked with our hands in a lovers' clasp on the straight towpath
  beside the canal that made us think
Of France, of tumbling autumn days, of hundreds and hundreds
  and hundreds of loves and visions.
Sometimes Cindy is half ill, sometimes more than half, because she
  doesn't know as much
As people she envies. She writes poems about not knowing, about the
  anguish over knowledge,
And when I was her age I felt the same way. I know well that anguish.
  I used to be pained especially
Because I could not name the colors I saw, and I envied painters their
  knowledge of pigments,
I studied the charts of colors and I looked up the names—mallow,
  cerise—in the dictionary,
I examined the meanings of *hue, shade, tone, tint, density, saturation,
  brilliance*, and so on,
But it did no good. The eye has knowledge the mind cannot share, which
  is why painters
So often are inarticulate. Is the eye ignorant, uneducated? How absurd.
  That would be impossible.
Hence I became eventually, gradually, unashamed of my mind's
  incapacity, just as I had once written
Poems to be read many times, but what was the use of that? Now I write
  poems to be read once and forgotten,
Or not to be read at all.

FRED CHAPPELL

Webern's Mountain

He felt the web of light tearing, the rainbow
Filaments from point to point detach
And quiver to invisibility
Like a newly discovered harmonic system at mercy
Of the State. Like an edelweiss dissected
With a bayonet. He felt it coming apart,
All of it at once coming apart;
And the time drew on again to climb the mountain.

The air was diamond-pure at these thin heights
Where nobility was forgotten and created.
The true nobility of perfect freedom,
The perfect nobility of true Idea.
He loved the ledges where no accident
Was possible without inhuman disaster.

SATOR AREPO TENET OPERA
ROTAS. *Keep the work circling*, keep the work
Contained, hermetic as fugue and involute
As the seashell lodged in the sky-lost precipice.
Might he not find among these terrible peaks
The flower that Goethe postulated, Ur-plant,
Theme for the infinite variations that greenly
Populate the world and all its mind?
The flower that from corolla to spidery root hair
Is but a single thought, a single wordchord.

Below the clouds the Fascists gathered their bundles
Of Jews and poets, preparing the clinical bonfire
That would cauterize the decadent suppuration,
Establish Ordnung for the blond millenia.

On Webern's mountain each row on row of rote tor
Was order consecrate by Origin,
Thematic figure etched upon a sky
That, arching, endlessly enclosed and opened it.

Then it came apart, the stave-line filaments
Of gleam snapped by mortar shell, viola
And cello strings dying under the tank treads.
And the lovely mountain fled to America,
The beautiful mountain that was Webern's father.

Message

For D.S.

True.
        The first messenger angel may arrive
purely clothed in terror, the form he takes
a swordblade of unbearable energies, making
the air he entered a spice of ozone.
And then, the mad inventories. Each force
of nature, each small animal and pretty bird,
is guilty with persistence. The tear of sorrow,
huge as an alien star, invades
our sun's little system.

                        Irrelevant,
such enormity: because the man is alone
and naked. Even the finely tenuous radiations

of the marauding star crush him like falling timbers.
The worst is, he must choose among sorrows
the one that destroys him most.
                                    But see how all
changes in that hour. He ascends
a truer dimension of event, he feels with senses
newly evolved the wide horizons unknown till now.
He is transformed head to foot, taproot to polestar.
He breathes a new universe, the blinding whirlpool
galaxies drift round him and begin to converse.

Forever Mountain

(J. T. Chappell: 1912–1978)

Beyond the scrub pine ridges, beyond Pisgah
With its bulged flank, behind the rood screen
Of new-leaved hickory hills, past Black Gap
That opens its vistas like a hand unclenching,
There is a deeper mist of mountains.

The tumbled mezzotint range unseen until this hour
Because the weather was too close.

But now a lofty smoke has cleansed my vision.

I see my father has gone to climb
Easily those slopes, taking the time
He's got a world of, making spry headway
In the fresh green mornings, stretching out
Noontimes in the groves of beech and oak.
He has cut a walking stick of second-growth hickory
And through the amber afternoon he measures

Its shadow and his own shadow on a sunny rock.
　　Not marking the hour, but observing
The quality of light come over him.
He is alone, except what voices out of time
Come to his head like bees to the beetree crown,
The voices of former life as indistinct as heat.

By the clear trout pool he builds his fire at twilight,
And in the night a granary of stars
Rises in the water and spreads from edge to edge.
He sleeps, to dream the tossing dream
Of the horses of pine trees, their shoulders
Twisting like silk ribbon in the warm breeze.

He rises glad and early and goes his way,
Taking by plateaus the mountain that possesses him.

My vision blurs blue with distance,
I see no more.
Forever Mountain has become a cloud
That light turns gold, that wind dislimns.

　　　This is a prayer.

JOHN CIARDI

It Is for the Waking Man
to Tell His Dreams

somnum
narrare vigiliantis est.
— SENECA

In the stupors before sleep
I used to hear in my head
poems at which God might weep,
each line an angel's bread.

They died awake, their myth
like the gold plates, God-bright,
Moroni brought to Smith
and then took back each night.

I wired my bed and taped
those oracles. Come day,
I heard: "The cat escaped
when Jesus ran away

with Mary's lamb, no doubt."
—And then a snore,
until the tape ran out,
the dog scratched at the door,

hearing its master's voice.
It is a dog's mistake
to wagtail and rejoice
because the fool's awake.

ALFRED CORN

Two Travelers on a Summer Evening

Unbroken stillnesses: the lake mist
Set for the night, an eggshell stratum
The pines bend and brace against.
Overhead has been stretched a panel
Less or more than sky, an
Unbounded, featureless null
The grain and bark-brown of aged silk.
—Under which, a temple in tiers (two, no, three)
Deep in the background and rightfully small,
With upcurving, cat's paw eaves,
And roofs the sort they always tile.
Crags. Low hills. Light falling. . . .
The human element here, a spindly next
To a thickset figure, almost escapes
Notice at first survey. Calligraphic, complex,
When magnified, they respond—starting with perhaps
The far one's hat, straw-golden, a conic section
He wears as shelter and emblem
(*Monk bearing staff*) of his calling.
Zeal urges him a pace beyond the factotum
(Freehand topknot, tense calves exposed)
Who makes steadily forward under a yoke—bamboo—
His arms looped up over the crossbar
With dangling bundles neatly matched
In a weight-to-weight correspondence.
Ten thousand invisible gnats.
A low frog gong from the lilypads expounds, expands. . . .
One footbridge (slatted); *two* rocks; *four* swallows.
The five, this time, fell out as barbed-wire **pines**;

(Standing, decidedly, for long life).
Weary travelers. But can they plausibly,
This muggy twilight, be very near their goal?—
The burnished image throned inside half smiling,
Its old beatitude a certainty
That pilgrims would be drawn there to the end of time.

She looks for them again in the lower right
Of the taut silk pane (a squared circle, corners rounded)
And tilts its gleaming stem back and forward,
Paddling aside flies (come here from where?) and gnats
In warm gusts around her armchair. Hangchou:
The Southern Sung. By the West Lake, at dusk,
Heaven-blessed, willow-crowded banks stir,
Sigh, and leave little to the imagination. . . .
There, according to the poet, (according to Lin-Chi),
"They forget their Southern exile,
And take Hangchou for K'ai-feng."

Prophet Bird

They found the earth mute and passionless and left.
—FRANK O'HARA

Your legend is still green with us, and avid
To demonstrate how you once scaled a mountain
Of orange-crates and "knocked them down," how simply
Lifting and lighting became the Promethean blaze. . . .
Now files of ants descend on their current
Windfall, gaining focus and perhaps a better grasp
Of the unlikely but all too portable whole,
Which you discarded in favor of newer stages,
Reluctant to lock up a plan next to its migrant
Double, the planetary warning, color of dried blood—

That impasse, too, was more than beginning
To dim and accept a kinder remnant of
Intention: the leaves turn when they fall.
We have our wishes for you still, the few
That find a rough-hewn, vine-covered lodging
For their chattels under the foothills near
Healing, variably heated springs. The ayes
And your hardly won singlings-out of praise
Befriend you for now, knowing you, enkindled
Early starling, first befriended them.

Naskeag

Once a day the rocks, with little warning—
not much looked for even by the spruce
and fir ever at attention above—
fetch up on these tidal flats and bars.
Large, crate-like rocks, wrapped in kelp;
layer on imprinted layer,
umber to claret to olivegreen,
of scalloped marbling. . . .
Not far along the path of obstacles
and steppingstones considered,
fluid skeins of bladder wrack
lie tufted over the mussel shoals—
the seabed black as a shag's neck,
a half-acre coalfield, but alive.
Recklessly multiple, myriads compact,
the small airtight coffers (in chipped enamel)
are starred over with bonelike barnacles
that crackle and simmer throughout the trek,
gravel-crepitant underfoot.

Evening comes now not with the Evening
Star, but with a breathing fog.
And fog is the element here,
a new term, vast by indefinition,
a vagrant damping of the deep tones
of skies and bars and sea.
Sand, mud, sand, rock: one jagged pool
basining a water invisible
except as quick trembles
over algal weed—itself
half-absent, a virid gel.
Walking means to lose the way
in fog, the eye drawn out to a farther point,
a dark graph on the faint blue inlet watershine;
out to where a heron stands,
stationing its sharp silhouette
against the fogbright dusk.
Then, not to be approached,
lifts off and rows upward, *up*, *up*,
a flexible embracing-forward on the air,
rising out of view
behind an opaque expanse of calcium flame.

The great kelp-dripping rocks,
at random positions,
lost in thought and dematerializing
with the gray hour,
release, indelibly, their pent-up contents.
—Even the scattered feathers here
are petrified, limewhite blades and stony down.
The sky, from eastward, deepens
with the dawning insight
as the seas begin to rise, the flats

slide away, the hulls bear off the ground,
and the eye alien to so self-sufficing
a tidal system turns and takes up how to
retrace the steps that brought it there.

CARL DENNIS

A Letter on the Lake

You don't know me but you must have seen me reading
On the dock facing yours across the inlet,
The gawky woman in the bright green straw hat
With plastic flowers, the neighbor
You never invited to your lawn parties,
Though not all your guests were graceful, I noticed,
And some were new-comers here, not friends.

Now that the season's over I can tell you
I think you lost as much as I have.
Others might have seen my flowery hat as a challenge
To reach beyond mere taste as their measure of the world,
To be true to the oath they swore when they were younger:
To teach when they couldn't learn;
To inspire when they weren't inspired.

You might have taken me out once on your boat.
When you spotted something far out on the water
And called to the crew, "Look there,"
I'd have looked the hardest.
I'd have been the one, seeing no cloud or sea speck,
To turn back to watch you,
Your eyes still fixed, arm still pointing,
Then dropping as a flag drops when the wind dies.

I'd have listened when you tried to explain
What it was; I'd have tried to picture it,
Something more vivid than a flag
Or sea cloud, more likely to live
Longer in memory, if not forever.

Looking at a Photograph on My Forty-Fourth Birthday

A dozen Amish men and women on the beach
In black suits and dresses, facing the water,
Their backs to the camera, fifty yards off.

They look out or down as if they've guessed that the waves
Rolling in endlessly have nothing to do
With the waves of wheat blowing on their fields.

A sea so empty that the only reason they can think of
For venturing on its gray Sahara is to reach home,
The traveler having been lured away by some trick.

A sailor trying ten years to get back to Ithaka
Would be easy for them to understand,
Not a sailor setting out for Troy.

And what would they say of a veteran after the war
Who had left no wife disconsolate ten years before,
No son to grow up fatherless on his own,

Whose sleep is unbroken by familiar cries for help
As he drifts in his skiff among islands, docking for a day,
Trading stories in the parks and the oyster bars?

Pen Pal

Other prisoners you've written to
Must have told you stories like mine,
How, when they were ten or eleven,
Their fathers began to drink too much,
How when the beatings grew too heavy
They ran loose all night.

I'm willing to admit that my brothers, as wild as I was,
Turned out all right. I don't compare
Their daily killings on the market now
With the one killing on my hands.

All I ask you to see is how much more hate
I had to keep in check than you had to
Or have to now, how good feelings,
When they come to you, come mostly from the heart,
Unforced, not from the will.
If I could write well,
I'd write a book on the subject of unequal chances,
Unequal tests and trials,   ———
And not mention myself at all.

The subject must interest you too.
Why else would you want to write me,
A stranger and a prisoner? I'm glad you do
In spite of the days when a bad taste rises in my throat
As I think how little anger you have to swallow
On waking each day in the sunlit, carpeted room
I imagine you waking in.
It's a full day's work for me not to envy
Your lack of envy for any man
As you look down on your garden.

In my best daydream I see myself down there
Among your friends, talking and laughing.
I'm watching a friendly game of croquet
And want to join in, but don't,
Afraid that the mallet in my hands
Might turn out dangerous, a missed shot
Stirring up something dark from the bottom
That for years had been slowly settling
Because I'd been holding my life still.

The Dream of Fair Women

Once when they came to my bed in dream
They came in the dark, nameless, bodies only.
Then they came in the light, faces visible,
Faces of women I could hope to encounter soon
If my luck changed, if I played my cards right,
Docked on the right islands, my face bronzed from the sea sun.
Now they come as the few women I've known well.

Is this a sign of the change I'm most afraid of,
The slow shifting of hope to memory?
They don't return as I remember them,
But older, as they might look now,
Their foreheads lined, dark hair crowded by gray.
One day their youth got up before dawn
And left them sleeping, and they woke up serious,
Not mournful, and saw from their window
That the mainland they called their home
Was in fact an island
With a single harbor seldom used.

In the way-station of my bed,
Their hands gripping my shoulders,
They tell their stories, saved up
Voyage after voyage for ears like mine.
However I listened before,
In my dream I listen carefully.
As I wake the words fade
But the tone lingers. As long as it lasts
Every story that I tell is true.

WILLIAM DICKEY

Three Songs

I. SONG OF THE BOWL OF FRUIT

The mother of composition, arrangement
at its best, little blue ribbons with gold
firsts and grands on them from the
Iowa State Fair, I dream
of the spheres and elongate egg-shapes
of artistic authority.

Think of the words Still Life
and how much they have meant to you
in times of personal chaos, times
when your hands and feet wept,
how the only thing comforting
was analytical cubism.

Plums, cherries, grave
elliptical Muscat grapes, the
eruption of figs splitting,
the lesser and greater constants, how
nothing, not even music, has the power
of a virginity of conclusions
about to be devoured.

II. SONG OF THE WASP

What this scene lacks is tonality,
the tight jitter and buzz,
disciplined flight of
formations of bombers arriving
to fertilize the tired cities,

salt wash of fear bringing
grandmothers and small children
together in the shadow of apprehension.
There is no elegance without death,
no beauty without using.

Time now to exercise the air,
which, if it is never ridden,
slumps lower and lower toward
the floor of the room, time
to alert the Rockingham cows
on the mantelpiece from their dream
of perpetual browsing, time
to remind this intolerable prose day
that wants only its own death, what
is the violence of punctuation.

III. SONG OF THE CHILD
HOME FROM SCHOOL

This room is round with self-confidence,
the very sofas congratulating
each other on their good taste, how
less is more, Confucius-the-Decorator told them.

I open my lunch box of Indians, who escape.
There are crumbs of salami sandwiches to distribute,
the smear of vitality, resonance
of one hundred and one thousand giggling condominiums.

I am only passing through here, and when
I have passed the sides of the room will clap together
like a burst brown paper bag. I am headed North
to the wild ice, where the big buck walruses are mating.

Hootali Ajignat

Do these words mean what I assume they mean?
Is there a man HOOTALI thinking AJIGNAT
or is there a mountain they are both climbing
being alternately the one climbed upon and the one climbing?

I am trying to work, here, under the dropcloths
representing the end of the world, with a machine
defined not as its shape but as its function.
In motion, I am that motion; out of motion
only a readiness. Not the house
that the gingerbread witch lives in and bakes and eats.

I think it is right in adolescence to believe in God
because we have to live in family and God is family.
But family falls away, towns disappearing
behind the moving train, then the train itself
becoming more skeletal until it is a hollow
train-shaped space moving in the space around it.

If I am that machine increasingly,
HOOTALI and AJIGNAT are manipulable.
It calls for the most careful exercise
of responsibility: to paint them without paint,
respecting the possibility that they could be painted.

Alas, children, you calling at Hallowe'en
in the guise of spirits, I have no physical gifts,
no candy skulls, no bitter chocolate coffins.
The end of the world is beyond death, death being a body.
The end of the world is irreversible, this machine
arranging itself to be and be in tomorrow.

Spider Web

There are stories that unwind themselves as simply
as a ball of string. A man is on a plane between
New York and Denver. He sees his life
as moving along a straight line. Today here,
tomorrow there. The destination is not so
important as the progression itself. During lunch
he talks to the woman seated beside him.
She is from Baltimore, perhaps twenty years older.
It turns out she has had two children killed
by drunk drivers, two incidents fifteen
years apart. At first I wanted to die everyday,
she says, now I only want to die now and then.
Again and again, she tries to make her life
move forward in a straight line but it keeps
curving back to those two deaths, curves back
like a fishhook stuck through her gut. I guess
I'm lucky, she says, I have other children left.
They discuss books, horses; they talk about
different cities but each conversation keeps
returning to the fact of those deaths, as if
each conversation were a fall from a roof
and those two deaths were the ground itself—
a son and daughter, one five, one fourteen.
The plane lands, they separate. The man goes off
to his various meetings, but for several days
whenever he's at dinner or sitting around
in the evening, he says to whomever he is with,
You know, I met the saddest woman on the plane.
But he can't get it right, can't decide whether

she is sad or brave or what, can't describe
how the woman herself fought to keep the subject
straight, keep it from bending back to the fact
of the dead children, and then how she would
collapse and weep, then curse herself and
go at it again. After a week or so, the man
completes his work and returns home. Once more
he gathers up the threads of his life.
It's spring. The man works in his garden,
repairs all that is broken around his house.
He thinks of how a spider makes its web,
how the web is torn by people with brooms,
insects, rapacious birds; how the spider
rebuilds and rebuilds, until the wind
takes the web and breaks it and flicks it
into heaven's blue and innocent immensity.

How to Like It

These are the first days of fall. The wind
at evening smells of roads still to be traveled,
while the sound of leaves blowing across the lawns
is like an unsettled feeling in the blood,
the desire to get in a car and just keep driving.
A man and a dog descend their front steps.
The dog says, Let's go downtown and get crazy drunk.
Let's tip over all the trash cans we can find.
This is how dogs deal with the prospect of change.
But in his sense of the season, the man is struck
by the oppressiveness of his past, how his memories
which were shifting and fluid have grown more solid
until it seems he can see remembered faces
caught up among the dark places in the trees.

The dog says, Let's pick up some girls and just
rip off their clothes. Let's dig holes everywhere.
Above his house, the man notices wisps of cloud
crossing the face of the moon. Like in a movie,
he says to himself, a movie about a person
leaving on a journey. He looks down the street
to the hills outside of town and finds the cut
where the road heads north. He thinks of driving
on that road and the dusty smell of the car
heater which hasn't been used since last winter.
The dog says, Let's go down to the diner and sniff
people's legs. Let's stuff ourselves on burgers.
In the man's mind, the road is empty and dark.
Pine trees press down to the edge of the shoulder.
Fixed in his headlights, the eyes of animals
shine like small cautions against the night.
Sometimes a trailer truck lit up like Christmas
roars past and his whole car briefly shakes.
The dog says, Let's go to sleep. Let's lie down
by the fire and put our tails over our noses.
But the man wants to drive all night, crossing
one state line after another and never stop
until the sun creeps into his rearview mirror.
Then he'll pull over and rest a while before
starting again, and at dusk he'll crest a hill
and there, filling a valley, will be the lights
of a city entirely new to him.
But the dog says, Let's just go back inside.
Let's not do anything tonight. So they
walk back up the sidewalk to the front steps.
How is it possible to want so many things
and still want nothing? The man wants to sleep
and wants to hit his head again and again
against a wall. Why is it all so difficult?
But the dog says, Let's go make a sandwich.

Let's make the tallest sandwich anyone's ever seen.
And that's what they do and that's where the man's
wife finds him, staring into the refrigerator
as if into the place where the answers are kept—
the ones telling why you get up in the morning
and how it is possible to sleep at night,
answers to what comes next and how to like it.

The Face in the Ceiling

A man comes homes to find his wife in bed
with the milkman. They're really going at it.
The man yanks the milkman off by his heels
so his chin hits the floor. Then he gets his gun.
It looks like trouble for all concerned.
Why is modern life so complicated?
The wife and milkman scramble into their clothes.
The man makes them sit at the kitchen table,
takes all but one bullet out of the gun,
then spins the cylinder. We'll let fate decide,
he says. For the sake of symmetry, he gets their
mongrel dog and makes him sit at the table as well.
The dog is glad to oblige but fears the worst.
North, south, east, west, says the man, who's the one
that God likes best? He puts the gun to his head
and pulls the trigger. Click. Whew, what a relief.
Spinning the cylinder, he aims the gun at his wife.
North, south, east, west, he says and again pulls
the trigger. Another click. He spins the cylinder
and aims at the milkman. North, south, east west.
A third click. He points the gun at the dog who is
scratching fitfully at his collar. North, south,
east, west, who do you think God likes best?

The man pulls the trigger. Bang! He's killed the dog.
Good grief, says the wife, he was just a pup.
They look down at the sprawled body of the dog
and are so struck by the mean-spiritedness
of the world's tricks that they can do nothing
but go out for a pizza and something to drink.
When they have finished eating, the man says,
You take my wife home, I'm sorry I was selfish.
And the milkman says, No, you take her home,
I'm sorry I was greedy. And the wife says,
Let's all go home together. A little later
they are lying side by side on the double bed
completely dressed and shyly holding hands.
They stare up at the ceiling where they think
they see God's face in the ridges of shadow,
the swirls of plaster and paint. It looks like
the kid who first punched me in the nose,
says the husband. It looks like the fellow
who fired me from my first job, says the milkman.
And the wife remembers once as a child
a man who called her over to his car,
and opening the door she saw he was naked
from his waist down to his red sneakers.
What makes you think that God likes anyone?
asks the wife. Wide awake, the three of them
stare at the ceiling trying to define the kind
of face they find there until the sun comes up
and pushes away the shadow and then it no longer
matters whether the face is good or evil, generous
or small-minded. So they get up, feeling sheepish,
and don't look at each other as they wash and
brush their teeth and drink a cup of coffee,
then go out and make their way in the world,
neither too badly nor too well as is the case
with compromises, sneaking along walls, dashing

across streets. You think it is nothing to risk
your life every day of the great struggle until
what you hold most precious is torn from you?
How loudly the traffic roars, how ferociously
the great machines bear down upon them,
and how courageous it is for them to be there.

RITA DOVE

A Hill of Beans

One spring the circus gave
free passes and there was music,
the screens unlatched
to let in starlight. At the well,
a monkey tipped her his fine red hat
and drank from a china cup.
By mid-morning her cobblers
were cooling on the window sill.
Then the tents folded and the grass

grew back with a path
torn waist-high to the railroad
where the hoboes jumped the slow curve
just outside Union Station.
She fed them while they talked,
easy in their rags. *Any two points
make a line*, they'd say,
and we're gonna ride them all.

Cat hairs
came up with the dipper;
Thomas tossed on his pillow
as if at sea. When money failed
for peaches, she pulled
rhubarb at the edge of the field.
Then another man showed up
in her kitchen and she smelled
fear in his grimy overalls,
the pale eyes bright as salt.

There wasn't even pork
for the navy beans. But he ate
straight down to the blue
bottom of the pot and rested
there a moment, hardly breathing.
That night she made Thomas
board up the well.
Beyond the tracks, the city blazed
as if looks were everything.

Wingfoot Lake

(Independence Day, 1964)

On her 36th birthday, Thomas had shown her
her first swimming pool. It had been
his favorite color, exactly—just
so much of it, the swimmers' white arms jutting
into the chevrons of high society.
She had rolled up her window
and told him to drive on, fast.

Now this *act of mercy*: four daughters
dragging her to their husbands' company picnic,
white families on one side and them
on the other, unpacking the same
squeeze bottles of Heinz, the same
waxy beef patties and Salem potato chip bags.
So he was dead for the first time
on Fourth of July—ten years ago

had been harder, waiting for something to happen,
and ten years before that, the girls
like young horses eyeing the track. Last August she stood
    alone for hours

in front of the T.V. set
as a crow's wing moved slowly through
the white streets of government.
That brave swimming

scared her, like Joanna saying
Mother, we're Afro-Americans now!
What did she know about Africa?
Were there lakes like this one
with a rowboat pushed under the pier?
Or Thomas' Great Mississippi
with its sullen silks? (There was
the Nile but the Nile belonged

to God.) Where came from
was the past, 12 miles into town
where nobody had locked their back door,
and Goodyear hadn't begun to dream of a park
under the company symbol, a white foot
sprouting two small wings.

STEPHEN DUNN

Completion

After the floor was grooved and tongued,
the walls panelled, windows framed,
a sadness came over him,
a wild sadness he did not resist.
It was close to elation
as if something melting in his shoulders
had reached his chest.
He wanted to dance.
He wanted to dial a neglected friend.
This was his room. Everything in it
he had wedged, fitted, nailed.
Outside, in the street and beyond,
was the world made by others,
fascinating, not to be trusted.
It always had called him,
and always he came.
His room seemed foolish, an umbrella
in a typhoon. It was done.
It certainly wouldn't do.
The sadness was all over him now.
He'd have a party, a bon voyage.
He could see himself breaking
a bottle on the hard, pitchpine floor.
Instead, he looked out the window.
He thought: the goddamn grass,
the goddamn leaves. A blue Toyota
passed. A red Dodge. It seemed comic
how much didn't belong to him.
When his wife returned from work

he said: Look, it's finished,
but he knew the room meant nothing
to her. His books would go in it,
his desk. Did his wife belong to him?
Could anyone *belong* to anyone else?
If neglected people weren't so sad
he would've called his neglected friend.
He was ready for that party again.
It would be evening, the indirect lighting
would confirm how careful he'd been
to keep the room peculiarly his.
He imagined his guests asking
about the switchbox. He imagined speaking
about the mitre work and joists,
the fluted moulding above the door.

A Birthday Gift

It's clear by now I'll never like
carpentry or yoga or those
politically correct, earnest people
who won't allow error in their lives.
It's the middle of my life,
the two or three things I'm good at
will have to do. No more guilt
for being unable to sustain love,
no more apprenticeships
before the humorless, no more
soul-work in the backwoods of Maine.
It's time to admit I never liked parades, that my disbelief
is never suspended at the opera,
that I've trouble speaking to people
fond of outer space.

I'm going to own up to loving T.V.,
insist few things are better than baseball
late in the season when everything counts.
It's too late to have anyone to dinner
who doesn't believe in charm.
I'm forty-four years old today!
I'll never play the guitar well.
I'll never change the awful world
and it's alright, this is the gift
to myself that says it's all right.
Hello loneliness, hello boredom,
I'm finally ready to make friends,
to give thanks for all
you've driven me to, to acknowledge
your rightful places near the heart.

At the Smithville Methodist Church

It was supposed to be Arts & Crafts for a week,
but when she came home
with the "Jesus Saves" button, we knew what art
was up, what ancient craft.

She liked her little friends. She liked the songs
they sang when they weren't
twisting and folding paper into dolls.
What could be so bad?

Jesus had been a good man, and putting faith
in good men was what
we had to do to stay this side of cynicism,
that other sadness.

O.K., we said. One week. But when she came home
singing "Jesus loves me,
the Bible tells me so," it was time to talk.
Could we say Jesus

doesn't love you? Could I tell her the Bible
is a great book certain people use
to make you feel bad? We sent her back
without a word.

It had been so long since we believed, so long
since we needed Jesus
as our nemesis and friend, that we thought he was
sufficiently dead,

that our children would think of him like Lincoln
or Thomas Jefferson.
Soon it became clear to us: you can't teach
disbelief to a child,

only wonderful stories, and we hadn't a story
nearly as good.
On parents night there were the Arts & Crafts
all spread out

like appetizers. Then we took our seats
in the church
and the children sang a song about the Ark,
and Halleleulah

and one in which they had to jump up and down
for Jesus.
I can't remember ever feeling so uncertain
about what's comic, what's serious.

Evolution is magical but devoid of heroes.
You can't say to your child
"Evolution loves you." The story stinks
of extinction and nothing

exciting happens for centuries. I didn't have
a wonderful story for my child
and she was beaming. All the way home in the car
she sang the songs,

occasionally standing up for Jesus.
There was nothing to do
but drive, ride it out, sing along
in silence.

RICHARD EBERHART

River Water Music

With the sun half way down the tall pines
Heading for the earth of Vermont,

I sit in New Hampshire high over the Connecticut
Listening, eskered, to electronic music expand,

High decibel, confronting nature with man's extravagance.
Power bursts of electronic music burst over the hills,

A kind of gigantic extravagance unknown to earlier ears
Which heard the rich slight wind whisperings of near sundown.

Brisk, strong, air-penetrating reverberances
Fan out into the innocent air for miles around,

Man denting the idea of ideal silence
With power gestures waking the ears to new feeling

While all over heaven flaunt the claps of electronic aggression
Saying the mind may be old but the sound is new.

The Mystical Beast in the Shadows

I saw it, the mystical beast in the shadows,
Unbelievable, but I believed it
Because I saw it, but I did not see it,
The eye could not fashion its passing.

Sitting erect, in complete control of myself,
Thinking of nothing, aware of everything,
At ten o'clock of an autumnal evening
An animal appeared at the side of the house,

Moved toward me, unconscious of me, came
Within twenty feet in the light from the porch
Extending across the lawn to darkness,
The animal turned, and crossed my vision.

Too swift an event for determination,
This beast, perfected in semi-darkness,
Came into vision and so swiftly left it
That I was astonished, and remained astonished.

It was real, not of my imagination,
But darkness obscured its furtive shape,
I will never know what assailed me,
Was it the soul of time oppressing my space?

Dead Skunk

I buried a skunk in the garden,
He was beautiful, dead on the lawn.
Nobody knows whether a dog or poison
Left him there in the beginning of Spring.

I purposely made his grave shallow
To keep him as near to life as possible,
Just barely under the stuff of the earth.
We should not bury death too deeply

But keep it as if with us.
This was a beautiful of God's creatures,

Striped body, black and white,
A white, conclusive tail.

I put a rock over the place
As if to say resolutely
I honor your life, I mark your death,
And know little of either.

White Pines, Felled 1984

Not one not dandled a man high up in the air,
A man in his prime, a spider on a steel line
One hundred feet up on a hundred year old pine,
If he'd miss just right the whine of the band-saw
He'd cut off his limb, the high man a dancer
Against the trunk, master of the slight hand signal
To the landed man on the marvelous machine,

In a minute a bright round spray of sawdust,
Like a stream of yellow life-giving juice,
Signals the downfall of a hundred year old tree,
Even one hundred and fifty, gone all, gone in
A jiffy as she topples in direction prescribed by
A rope tensed to a tree down hill down a slope,
She snaps off just right and lands with a big bang.

The end of tree makes thud-rumble, moves the earth.
A line of magnificent white pines, one got out of line,
Snapped thirty feet from the top in a high wind,
Landed on my neighbor's garage, ruined his portico,
If it had snapped half down or more it would
Have creased the whole white house from attic to cellar,
Perhaps struck his eighties old mother moveless inside.

We knew what we did when delved or hewed,
Racked and crashed the growing green, rational with
A saving ritual so that not our house next door
Should be cleaved by a two-ton tree in a tricky wind,
Perhaps end us in our house, these things of beauty
Growing a foot a year become things of danger. Thirty
Years of beauty might produce life-crash, instant death.

When beauty is dangerous a man can dandle
Himself up high on a hundred foot white pine tree,
Able, without emotion, rational, the old tree at his
Lack of mercy and delicate materialistic apt know-how.
When beauty is dangerous top the tree, then bring
her down in resounding earth-wallop. Aftercomers
Serve cocktails from the beauty of the elegant stump.

The Angels

Some angels were standing on the ground
Unable to fly, their wings extended upward.

They kept this stance and pose year after year.
They were made of marble, unable to be human.

These creatures dazzled the ambient Florida sunshine,
Stood immaculate on the ground and never moved.

They looked like perfection, to be eyed askance
Driving by year after year. Nobody would buy them.

They kept their residence near the lake,
I fisherman came by with big ruddy looks,

Went to the lake and took out a boat.
Green slime and blue water and white sky

Were all in motion when hook and mouth met,
The thrashing resplendent as the man hauled in

A big bright color of life for breakfast, and kept
Fishing all day in the belief of muscle and tone.

The white marble angels were always there, though,
Nobody would buy them, they could not move,

They were perfect and viewed life without expression.
When you passed them you looked but could not think a word.

I never forgot them they were so unexpected,
Breath-taking, out of this world, caught in it.

A decade does nothing to them. Nobody would
Buy them. Their marble wings never got off the ground.

They saw me age as I came by another year,
Took out a boat, went on the orange and weedy water

And caught the fish struggling to gasp for air
With no hope, giving his life for my breakfast,

Muscle and tone, while the angels were standing useless,
Unviolated, unable to fly, I thought to buy one

But what would I do with a stiff, marble, non-creature
So resolutely sub and super human, so final,

So far away from my desires and aspirations,
No suffering, no pain and joy, nothing for breakfast.

JOHN ENGELS

Revisit

The clear disk of the sun
was dim on the horizon as the moon.
I could by its light discern
less than prospect, for nothing

described itself except
it was rendered out of loss
or loneliness. In my tracks
the snow smoked and swirled

as if fire were on the verge
of breaking through.
Light had begun to penetrate
the ice on the windows,

to drift over the floors,
climb slantingly the walls.
I imagined how in late afternoon
it might free itself once more

to the bitter yard
from which I should by then
have been for hours gone—
though for the moment it sustained

the deep, familiar rubbles
of emptiness. In the wintry yard
I stood to reclaim right
of property, and looked

up at the windows, one of which
I recalled to have opened
onto the fragrance
of the lavender lilac, the other

onto that of the white.

Orchard

By late afternoon the light
had given way and the air
had cooled. Mists
welled from the warm ditches,

spilled over and merged.
We drove through the topmost
layers of a growing cloud.
From the doorsills up our house

greeted us, though directly enough
we found the steps and walked
sure-footed in, the rooms
settling a little as we entered—this

after a gilt September day
in usual celebration of itself
spent picking apples
in the Yellow Delicious orchard,

the air beneath the young trees
a dust of green light, the apples
fragrant and scattered windfall
so that wherever we looked

(our glasses streaked, everything
blurring and unfocussed)
there seemed to have occurred
in the orchard grass among

the strict rows of the trees
an exuberant error
of the season, a great
and sudden yield of yellow flowers.

Goldfinch

After the goldfinch
had in a spark of panic
flown, the stalk of timothy
went on shivering

for longer than ordinary,
for there was wind
by reason of which overnight
the world had given way

by half at least, the trees
nearly bare, the woods
admitting a good
measure of light.

As for the goldfinch,
nothing remained, excepting
the small impulse it had lent
the grass, sustained far longer

than one moved
to consider so small
an evidence of breath might
rightly have expected.

Cardinals in the Ice Age

When Alice called to say
a pair of cardinals was at her feeder,
and that they'd been around for days,
I was, besides envious, reassured,

not having at my own tray seen
in years a cardinal; had grown in fact
to fear I might not soon again;
had thought they must have fled

the growing inclemencies of this place
to somewhere further south; and it was clear
I had not the strategies to lure them north
again. To me it was in the way of a most

considerable loss. But here were cardinals,
or at least word of them, and any time I chose
I might cross the road and see them for myself;
and yet stayed home, for while it was a short walk,

the day was cold, the road a difficult course
of icy ruts, and they were not my cardinals
but Alice's. Besides, was it not enough to know
the birds were back, there in my neighbor's yard,

blood-like against the vivid snow? I took this
to be rare and necessary evidence that still
some time was left before the first lobes
of the great oncoming ice in its long probe south

would awaken the neighborhood one night
to the sounds of our mountains going down,
screech of rock on bedrock, huge
morainal wave of houses, trees and boulders,

and then the dull moon reflecting
from the face of the ice-cliff
that will loom two miles overhead
into a birdless sky.

DONALD FINKEL

Waiting for the Wind

Wind wafts his fitful
    dispensations—incense,
        wren-song, distant bells.
We reach to catch them.
    As soon catch a cloud
        in a fish-net,
rain in a teaspoon.
    Now he's playing
        with the jacaranda,
rumpling her leaves
    with his clumsy fingers,
        parting her limbs
like slim brown thighs.
    Now he's dragging
        that disreputable nimbus
across the morning's lips
    like a dirty handkerchief.
        Now it's back in his pocket.
Not a breath of rain.

Oracle

Rain on the reservoir,
    water on water,
        a hexagram for good fortune.

Southwest,
                behind a pearl-grey scrim,
                      something's muttering.
The campo twitches its dusty hide
                    and the mesquites twitter.

Overhead
            the sky winks at us
                    through cracks in the cloud deck.
A cool gust
           flings the first few
                coins of rain
on the sun-stunned bricks.
           Where there was little
                there's a little more.

Crumbs

As I come hulking
           round the corner,
                a lizard wakes,
skittering
           through the bougainvillaea,
                her shadow caught
like an iron-grey lash
           in the corner of sight.
                  How long had she lain there,
the leathery nymph,
           sunning on the chapel wall,
                waiting for the wind
to drop her a cropful
           of bitter crumbs
                from his high table?

Round the blooming maguey,
                    hummingbirds creak
                              like tiny doors.
They hold their course
                    by constant flight.
                              She keeps her hold
by letting go.
          Eternities
                    of tireless ardor,
          diminishing intervals
                    of repose.

Enough

Two weeks of rain,
                    reservoir creeping through the early corn,
taking the campo back from the campesinos.
                    This morning the sun
thrusts his rough tongue through the alto-stratus
                    and licks my tiller hand.

We're riding west again,
                    brick gunwales breasting the zephyrs,
a full set of bedsheets and dishcloths
                    rigged from the chimney
                              to catch the faintest breath,
C humming below in the garden,
                    tying back the bougainvillaea,
                              sheafs of veined magenta bloom
on our stone transom,
                    hummingbirds creaking in the halyards,
                              lizard rubbing her back on the keel.

JORIE GRAHAM

Self Portrait As Both Parties

1.

The cut flowers riding the skin of this river.

2.

Dallying, dallying, wanting to go in.

3.

Wanting to be true, at the heart of things but true.

4.

Imagine the silt and all that it was.
The grains that filter down to it through the open hands of the sunlight.
How its rays weaken down there. How when it comes to touch
that smoothest of animals the slow bottom of the river
is it Orpheus as it glides on unharmed but really
turned back with its one long note that cannot
break down?

5.

How would he bring her back again? She drifts up
in a small hourglass-shaped cloud of silt where the sunlight touches,
up to where the current could take her
up by the waist into the downstream motion again into the
hard sell and for a moment even I can see
the garment of particles which would become her body
swaying, almost within reason, this devil-of-the-bottom,
almost yoked again almost quelling her weightlessness,
flirting here now with this handful of
mudfish his fingers touch silver. . . . But they gun

6.

through the weeds, the weeds cannot hold her
who is all rancor, all valves now, all destination,
dizzy with wanting to sink back in
thinning terribly in the holy separateness.
And though he would hold her up this light all open hands
seeking her edges seeking to make her palpable again
curling around her to find crevices by which to carry her up,
flaws by which to be himself arrested and made,
made whole, made sharp and limbed, a shape,
she cannot, she cannot the drowning is too kind,
the becoming of everything which each pore opens to again,
the possible which each momentary outline blurs into again,
too kind too endlessly kind
the silks of the bottom rubbing their vague hands
over her forehead, braiding her to

7.

the sepulchral leisure, the body, the other place which is not minutes,

8.

from which he searches he searches which is his majesty

9.

all description all delay this roundabout the eye must love.

Ravel and Unravel

I think I understand today how she could come to love it best,
the unravelling, Penelope, every night,
the hills and cypress trees turning back
into thread, then patience again, then . . .
is it emptiness?
All the work of the eyes and breath and fingertips that forced
    the two dimensions down
into each other going now, all of an instant, back
to what other
place?
Because we were lost, taking our time, today,
taking the long way back
from looking for the Indian petroglyphs we knew were there
but couldn't find, alone in the miles, the wind
kissing the rocks
to translate them down.
You walked ahead, navigating, lost one, carrying
Emily, all cargo now that I
am emptied finally
of all but my own
undoing
like the sun rising over these gigantic rock formations
coming to touch, in time, every millimeter
of every declivity, rounding, pronouncing them
into the emptiness.
So that I don't know if the cry was one I heard or
realized, clinging to the windy unsaid as it did,
hovering in, and diving madly from, the possible, the poverty,
wild, high-pitched, mewing and hissing and
knifing down
from two young eagles
into the heart.
They dove they rose,

as helpless on the draft as in control.
Was it the sky's? Was it my listening silting in?
It was the cry where play and kill are one.
It made me hear how clean the sky around them was of
anything I might have trapped it with.
So when I heard her crying up ahead,
pulling me in,
I heard her cry not add itself
to this enclosure of an emptiness
growing more empty as the minutes flick. I heard
how it stood for strength and was not of that strength.
Unlike that screech, that ancient breath
without a shape above me it
was desire.
I could hear how she and her cry went separate ways,
one to be lost one to be wholly
found out, word for word, taking the place of the sky, a violent
    usefulness. . . .
Because there is a moment which is the mother. It flicks
open, alive,
here and *here* though here she's
clothed she's
already gone, only siren, kingdom without extension,
secret sexual place of
placelessness.
Her body opens, burns,
at the edge of each rock each cliff
where the dust is pulling free,
wild in the air again
momentarily,
all arms, the light touching round each mote each grain again, alive,
more than
alive. . . .
Then the beautiful, the view all round us, with that crimp of use in it,
then the husband minutes bearing down, bearing down.

MARILYN HACKER

Corona

For Kim Vaeth

You're flying back, weighted with half the books
that piled the work-table and the night-table.
They bulk your rucksack. You gum on a label,
consign it, while our eyes condense three weeks'
talk, silence, touch: relief, regret. It looks
like complicity. Friends, with a third friend,
I put my hand on your nape; you put your hand
in my back pocket. I kiss, first, both cheeks,
surprise you on your mouth. Your flight's called. I
watch you, helmed with departure, stubborn, brave
in cream shirt, lilac trousers, suede shoes, tie
the next tan, turn, glisten, go. Concave
space takes you, the cord's cut. We leave. I crave
uncomplicated quiet, and the sky.

Uncomplicated quiet, and the sky
a Marian mantle through the car window.
I think of all the things I'll never know.
"I wish I was older," the young girl said. "Why?"
"So I would know more." You and she and I
spanned twenty years among us. While you drove
serpent curves through vineyards and olive groves,
she read *The Bell Jar*, till we stopped to buy
Chianti at a *cave*, upturned the bell
to shining tulips where the garnet wine
perfumed our morning. Weight in the palm, see, smell,

taste: our three mouths contemplated fine
meditations of ancient earth, as well
considered as just measures for a line.

Considered as just measures for a line,
sound more than sense determines words I choose;
invention mutes intention. If the shoes
you bought were grey suede clogs, size thirty-nine,
if we sang passion's matins and compline,
I'm story-telling. Reading poetry
we expect truth, you said, and I agree.
Truth, in particulars, I can define.
They're brown, your oxfords, and size forty-one;
two nuns, watching over another nun
through a night of fever, could not have kept
their limbs more ordered than we did; we slept
apart, together: facile franchise, whose
unsubtle truth can blanket subtlety.

Unsubtle truth can blanket subtlety.
In the next room, you slept in our guest-friend bed.
Where I wrote, your pad sat, pen-marked. I read
that morning, what, that night, you'd thought of me.
I wished I could evaporate, could be
anywhere else. I thought "Ingratitude,"
and flinched, while Tuscan light ignored my mood.
If I fail friendship, what felicity
left? Words crystallize despite our lives, select
emblems from hesitations and suspect
feelings. I coaxed your questioning, oblique,
till words undid what they had done. We speak
our pieces: peace. Plural, and amical,
we crossed the Arno, walked beyond the wall.

We cross the Arno, walk beyond the wall
up a steep wooded hill I climbed before
with another woman, hand in hand.
Now we hold hands, too, meaning something more
and less than "sex". At the ramparts, we stand
looking down sungilt waves of clay roof-tile
tender in late light slanted, now, toward Fall.
We separate ourselves from day-trip style
tourists, though we are tourists after all.
We need a breather from the personal.
Facts permit us touch. You rest your head on
my lap while I praise Suzanne Valadon.
Fatigue relaxes to repose in your
tanned shoulders, opulent and muscular.

Tanned shoulders, opulent and muscular,
power exuberant strokes. The choppy lake
frames, then conceals, your dolphin play. You take
a deep breath and submerge, then surface, far
away, all shining. There's a rectangular
concrete slab on pillars we saw boys make
lolloping dives from. You swim to it, break
thigh-high from the water, stretch to it, are
pendant by your wet arms, straining to pull
yourself up by them, drop, splash, leap again
determined from the water, less playful
now, challenged. You fall back. After ten
tries, you heave your leg over, stand, know I've
watched. I photograph your offhand dive.

Watched, I photograph your offhand dive.
How to depict attention that surveys
ground for reflexive confidence. Delays
are legion. When I navigate, you drive
home that indecision makes you arrive
exhausted anywhere. The hand belays

the rope to you's not mine. After a day's
mileage, Motown, nineteen-sixty-five;
we sing the car the last dark miles: "You can't
hurry love." We're almost what's almost home
to me. The constellated coast invokes
those road blues I'll sing myself, revenant
on airport buses when, again alone,
I'm flying back, weighted with half the books.

April Interval I

Wherever I surface I reinvent
some version of the Daily Walk to Town:
two miles rewarded with an hour's browse round
the market square or its equivalent:
a yard sale off the Dyer County Road
Rua Visconde de Pirajá.
Company is unwanted as a car.
I have, I've found, an operative code.
Perhaps, at forty, I'm escaping Nurse
Conscience to look for Mother in the shops;
perhaps irregularities, slow stops,
burst-starts of footfall echo feats of verse.
Perhaps it's just that I procrastinate
incorrigibly, as I've always done,
justified by a footpath splashed with sun.
Precipitation is precipitate.
Now I'm an orphaned spinster with a home
where spoils of these diurnal expeditions
can be displayed in prominent positions.
I'll hang this crazy-quilt in the front room,
its unembarrassedly polychrome
velvet rhomboids and uneven satin
patches lined with fancy-work, no pattern

twice. She painted flowers and leaves on some
a hundred years ago. I know it's "she."
"The life," at my age, will only be "sweet"
as I make it. I can't guarantee
myself a Boston marriage or more money,
but I can be outdoors and on my feet
as long as I'm still sound, and it's still sunny.

Queen Charming

For Alice, a revision

A woman writing thinks back through her mothers
—VIRGINIA WOOLF

Dear Godmother,—Another year, time for the Rendezvous
Ball rolls round again. There's my me-too pumpkin
Taxi at the door just aching to tick-tock me through
The ivory-inlaid-with-horn bulwarks for a little spin

Around the countryside, a royal good-will tour
Of the village, a stop in the street I used to call home.
The blue plaque tacked up beside a certain door
Embarrasses me. In the old days it wasn't a slum.

Everyone there was dressed quite respectably
Except for me. I want to tell them even then I was special,
I stood out. In the midst of such common extremity,
How should I have been distinguished by you from all

The rest? Those Pega-soused rodents and twitchy footmen
You improvised for my debut in the top-flight addled *onus*
Non probandi pageantry of clod and swell still run
Loose in my pasture of nightmares, more real than dailiness.

I want you to know I am mindful of the continuation
Of your gifts, wrapped up or unwrapped with your brisk
Senses of humor and limit, though my scantling maiden
Nickname still flutters in the dark, recherché whisk,

A rhythmic shushing of ash around my heart, driven
By the fare-meter's motor, in tune to the seedy axle
That brought me to, but not quite back from, Exception.
Now my royal pseudo-, or is it alternym, is all

I need to lift me from a tangled bed as the coupé
Pumpkin takes to the air in streaks, and I hear the King
About to knock on my door with the breakfast tray.
He is such a sweetie, really; I have nothing

To complain of there, unless it is the unremitting
Kindness of such an idiosyncratic custom.
I wiggle my toes, still almost numb from dancing
The night away in the old hallucinatorium,

Still half-slippered in their confection of solid tears.
These soft pedals must kick free for the daily round,
Prosaic in its way as the shining tea that pours
In a steady stream of miraculous glitters, strained

To absolute clarity, golden as silence, yet to be
Rightly clouded. Milk or lemon? I stare into my cup.
A sprinkle of dark leavings—mice? Ghost's breath glimmery
On the surface—mother?—I'm going . . . I look up.

The King has kissed me good morning, as usual,
And whispered something—perhaps he reminded me
Of certain things I must see to—before the Ball.
What was it—the food, decorations, last-minute charity?

I must drink this down, get up and get dressed.
Put on my manners, my face, my workaday coronet.
All day I'm Queen, and charming, but . . . you know the rest.
By midnight, I'm dumped right back into the ashbucket,

Rags and all. But of course you know. All over again,
You appear at the garden's edge, and call me softly;
Again I swallow discredit and fetch the unlikely pumpkin,
Find my sooty creepmouse dress replaced with finery,

Watch mice evolve to power as you put the harness to
Their tiny hack capacities. Everything you do to disguise
Me, right down to the oddity of the transparent shoe,
Is supposed to make me more or less myself, I guess.

But which? Could I endure without the punctual
Nightmare, the return? The retrospects of sorting
Ashes from lentils, salt-watering the crooked hazel
To keep the breeze green over Mother's grave, fighting

The rituals of narcissism every hint of rejection
Demands, re-cindering my nest—does all this improve
My character as you would wish, or simply put it on
Simmer forever, on the stern-most burner of the stove?

Is it possible to unforesee the midnight
Dishabille, or hold no regular moratorium
On masquerade? Despite a number of years and credit
Between broad satin sheets, the rescue remains phantom

As the windfall of a sunrise reprieve to a felon
Convicted of killing the child she was expecting
To be, forever . . . This is not clear. You know what I *mean*,
If anyone does. There is more than one ghost hanging

About my vanity for its chance. My weird sisters cut
Off their toes and heels for this. Why am I chosen,
Who did nothing but comfort myself, dragging my feet
With self-pity, to pay homage to the imaginary woman

Buried with my mother's bones? Those lucky doves
In the hazel branches looked after me fairly well,
Seeing what a mess I was. They tell me everybody loves
A self-effacer. Say, does your whole clientele

Keep coming back this way, after you've sent them out
Feet first into the fitting rooms? Do they come clean,
Change in time, toss out the frowzly petticoat,
Keep ashes out of the soup for good and dream

Too deeply to remember? Do the humiliating pangs
Of separation ever soften? Today we hold an audience,
The King and I, for all our subjects—their hopes, harangues,
Tragic or funny stories, grievances; and then the dance.

Are you sending someone to dance with my grown son?
I shall tell her "nothing is promised"; she'll be thinking
I am the expected witch, until she sees the whole design.
All who chance to enter into the state of Charming

Come to see the tricks involved, in time, evolved. I do
Not promise, as any Young Thing will think she can,
To deserve what has been given, or to be true
To her future, to efface her past. I do maintain

A possible grace, my humor, my figure, my face
Lifted, to thank you, to keep everything in its proper place.
                    As never,
                    Your Cinderella

A Poem Not about a Zebra

For Nat-le-Beau, a.k.a. The Insight Lady

If you want to psychoanalyze this high-
minded form of ungulate, don't try
to start with her heart which pumps harder,
for the same mundane results, than any other.
You'd do better to see her upside-down
Arc de Triomphe moss-velvet crown,
or the convex mystic coffee eye-cups,
the crazy salad fingered by her lips,
or coat the color of over-ripest mangos,
patched like moving sunlit sandstone patios.

You must agree her outside in-
ability to speak or grin
does not deny her personality
a most transcendent sort of superficiality:
camouflage counts heavily when you are odd.
Forget the heart, the cartilege, and God.
Forget the inner truths, the dark, and Tweedledee.
There is absolutely no identity

except in what makes one, particularly, laugh
or weep as, particularly,
                                        a giraffe.

Woman with Gardenia: a sketch

For Breda, posing for the "life class"

There is a point beyond which the human image refuses to play ball.
Its structure has a terrible lack of acquiescence toward the pun and
the decorative. — RICO LEBRUN

She looks so simple—a gardenia
In her hair—to draw, to get down
Simply; no tricky cuff, belt, blouse,
Or fold of fashion to come between
My eyes and the subtle quirks of her pose.
Nothing between the disposable porous
Paper and the nose of my conté crayon;
The flimsy surface might be skin—I'll draw that close.
        Still, there's awe.

I'm told some lines are more stable
Than others—the straight up-and-down,
Or horizontal—and the others will move
Toward rising, or falling, or even to tears;
And when, in drawing, push comes to shove,
Your free-hand curves,—so quick to love
Themselves thoughtlessly, and forget Hers,—
Are best controlled. Go slow, or you will prove
        False, and fail.

She is not that simple, not afraid to be
Silly putty on our sub-vellum, put hastily down
As freakishly deformed somehow—headless,
Footless, too fat, unbalanced, oddly quaint
Or over-athletic. She assumes our carelessness.
She holds still, knowing she must always
Be mistaken, drawn through point by point
Departures from her true appearance, what she alone *is*,
        Perfectly.

How can she keep it up? To draw
The warm gesture of her reaching down
Across her torso, as if to hold out
An invisible apple, takes more time
Than I could have imagined. To start,
Her whole body's balanced with the weight
Of that sly hand. And then you see the same
Curve reversed in a leg, or echoed, each part . . .
                    Gardenia?

"I want basic volumes, mass and form;
I want planes; get the primary down,
Then secondary. I don't want to see
Any belly-button, nipple, shadow, scar—
A lousy cake, with frosting, is still lousy—
Got it?" I do. I'm wearing wool, and she
Must be freezing, with nothing but a flower
(I can't add now—not to a fumbled body)
                    To keep her warm.

"Every line," we hear, "must aspire to be
Specific. Don't be looking down
Expecting your own mess to tell you what does
Or doesn't go; keep looking at the model.
Each single mark you make should stress
Committment to Her; the less you look at her, the less
True the figure. How often do I have to tell
You: *sorta ain't good enough!*" Now, this is
                    Not easy.

How does it feel, to hold her pose, to have
Your ankle grasp your foot, *that* way, go down
In tendon, nerve; or have your rib jut past
Your hip in sexy contraposto

Exaggeration? How does your hand feel, pressed—
Lightly or tightly—against her iliac crest?
Which muscle in our arms might show?
I need the capability known best, at most,
                    As negative.

I do not have it yet. Maybe
I never will. It is really getting me down,
All this scribbling, random as weather,
Passing as the fragile bloom of gardenia,
Cloud-headed, foot seldom in touch with a floor
I know is there . . . Why can't I keep her
In line? It helps not one iota
To measure the distances, figure, honor
                    Geometry.

How long does it take to grow—the idea
Glitters—a body both up and down
To where it may be improved by nothing
But a single frosting of gardenia? How long
Did it take her to grow that flower, watering,
Watching, before it was ready for wearing
Here today? Is it right or wrong
For me to stare at it 'til you are offering
                    Your gardenia?

And I am taking it home—that simple
Thing that could not be drawn, let down
Like Art, or hair, or aspiring Inspiration;
In place of a decent drawing, I have
This, this difficult fascination
She needed to wear to come between
(As if she knew) me and her execution. I love
Distraction more than Truth, if it be known
                    As Awe. Still . . .

The Case of Ample Ora: Sweetness and Light

Take me for example: I am no dumb belle
anxious to make a muscle, nor your brassy one
hung up and *so* dependent, a mammose shell
skirting pure air plus that tongue hung down
to my hem made mainly to wag for a meal;
yet I may offend in my way of being a body
builder, or in the mindless way I call
attention to my self, the emergency
of hunger, fire, the Sunday service, time
or a gain in the market, making my roundness sound.

Such likeness is coincidence, the rhyme
of surfaces, and senseless. Pound for pound,
I make more sense than commonly is thought.

Concerning fat: It's plain to see. I am
pap in a sack, a joke, jampacked, an out-
law, a gobbledegirl . . . I tip the beam
at four-oh-eight and dress in a tablecloth,
colossal, lackbrain, jolly, a real scream,
a ton of tidbits, genius of slop and sloth,
abundance in a bubble . . . What a crime
against the fit!

                    But get this straight: the round
Venus harks from the glacier's edge, the nigh
sugarplum of hardship, moonship. All round
was necessity.

Those were the days when I
was beautiful, with no need to redeem
my flab with a blab complex, to defend that cell
where sweetness and light are bound to serve their time
like money in the bank.

Fat is my fuel,
more metaphormorphic than the simpler tissues
of bone and muscle, mother of my nerve,
cushion of identity, its issues
more burning. Heavy matters. I deserve
some credit—I am no less than a gross
national product.

I accrete, a model
of growth, exchange; I can vamp up a loss,
a good stock figure, laughing, living well
within my lipid means, conglomerate,
exemplary as the ship of state, its trades
ballasted with freedom, sailing out
low-bellied with Ritz crackers and warheads,
well worth its weight in guilt . . .

All this, and no
one bends a knee to my avoirdupois,
though some heads bow in passing to bestow
invisibility upon me, qua
kindness. *Do* spare me that. Admit I am
a presence, even ungainsayable
as the memory in everyone's cytoplasm
of widespread famine, powerful oracle.

My Rorschach's boring. I see butterflies
or trees or clouds. But show me a genuine
piece of cake—I'll launch you fantasies
equal to Grimm, with oral rapes and ten
other ways to have it, eat it, bare
my voracic whole, so bored and boring
deeper. Right to the heart that pimps desire
to the hilt, my hypothalamus glowing
with glucose, molecular charmer, her gnomic
sugars a push in my ear, a breezy hum
in my mouth like a tongue of tides to flick
my whole insides awake with salty rhythm
and foamy titters . . .

         Ample Ora, take me
for ex-ample, please, I'm all I say
I am: the words are a body—of sorts—but weigh
nothing, nothing . . .

         My nothing is heavy;
I must make light of it, I must be jolly,
for laughter has no body—like me—the invisible
behind the heft, the lips that open to be
sweet, to be light, to rise, able after all to smile.

The Vision of Marsden Hartley

Night is coming to the islands
of Maine, pine-shouldered
in their smouldering slack;
the sea with the smoke of a mountain
breaks the mirror of Katahdin.

To the gull with closed eyes,
drowned among bottles and combs,
this greyness of wing
and breast and cheek
washed in the cold salt shallows.

Night is coming to the chalked houses
with their plain drawn blinds.
And to the people
grown quiet in their rooms
without lamps or shadows,
seated and staring,
hands on their heavy knees.

The night that Ryder knew—
great, molten wave
with all its sea-lights burning.

A cold and sweating horse
gallops inland from the wreck
of Time, overturning
as he runs, salt of pillars
and paint of stalls . . .

To the pale, muted track
where Death is riding,
and all the trees are white.

1980–84

From the Workshop of Brancusi
and Giacometti

Nothing bestial or human remains
in all the brass and tin
that we strike and break and weld.

Nothing of the hand-warmed stone
made flesh, of the poured heat
filling breast, belly and thigh.

The craft of an old affection
that called by name the lion shape
of night, gave rain its body

and the wind its mouth—The owl
in the mask of the dreamer,
one of the animal stones asleep . . .

—By tinker and by cutting torch
reduced to a fist of slag,
to a knot of rust on a face of chrome.

So, black dust of the grinding wheels,
bright and sinewy curl of metal
fallen beneath the lathe:

Speak for these people of drawn wire
striding toward each other
over a swept square of bronze.

For them the silence is loud
and the sunlight is strong.

No matter how far they walk,
they will never be closer.

1981–84

Ancestor of the Hunting Heart

—after Breugel

There is a distance in the heart
and I know it well—
a somberness of winter branches,
dry stubble scarred with frost,
late of the sunburnt field.

Neither field, nor furrow,
nor woodlot patched with fences,
but something wilder: a distance
never cropped or plowed,
only by fire and the blade of the wind.

The distance is closer than
the broomswept hearth—
that time of year when leaves
cling to the bootsole,
are tracked indoors,
lie yellow on the kitchen floor.

Snow is a part of the distance,
cold ponds, and ice
that rings the cattle-trough.

Trees that are black at morning
are in the evening grey.
The distance lies between them,
a seed-strewn whiteness
through which the hunter comes.

Before him in the ashen snow-litter
of the village street
an old man makes his way,
bowed with sack and stick.

A child is pulling a sled.

The rest are camped indoors,
their damped fires smoking
in the early dusk.

1983

DONALD HALL

The Henyard Round

1.

From the dark yard by the sheep barn the cock crowed
to the sun's pale
spectral foreblossoming eastward in June,
crowed,
　　　and crowed,
later each day through fall and winter, conquistador
of January drifts, almost-useless vain strutter
with wild monomaniac eye, burnished swollen chest,
yellow feet serpent-scaled, and bloodred comb,
who mounted with a mighty flutter
his busy hens: Generalissimo Rooster
of nobody's army.
　　　　　When he was old we cut his head off
on the sheepyard choppingblock, watching his drummajor
prance, his last resplendent march . . .
As I saw him diminish, as we plucked each feathery badge,
cut off his legs, gutted him,
and boiled him three hours for our fricasse Sunday
dinner, I understood
How the Mighty are Fallen, and my great-uncle Luther,
who remembered the Civil War,
risen from rest after his morning's sermon, asked
God's blessing on our food.

2.

At the depot in April, parcel post went cheep-cheep
in big rectangular cardboard boxes, each
trembling with fifty chicks. When we opened

the carton in the cool toolshed
fifty downed fluffers cheep-cheeping
rolled and teetered.
                              All summer it was my chore
to feed and water them.
Twice a day I emptied a fouled pan
and freshened it from the trough; twice a day
I trudged up hill to the grainshed, filled
sapbuckets at wooden tubs and poured
pale grain into v-shaped feeders, watching the greedy
fluster and shove.
                        One summer
I nursed a blind chick six weeks—pale yellow,
frail, tentative, meek,
who never ate except when I gapped space for her.
I watched her grow little by little,
but every day outpaced
by the healthy beaks that seized feed
to grow monstrous—and one morning
discovered her dead: meatless, incorrigible . . .

                              3.

At summer's end the small roosters
departed by truck, squawking with reason. Pullets
moved to the henhouse and extruded each day
new eggs, harvested morning and night. Hens roosted
in darkness locked from skunk and fox,
and let out at dawn footed the brittle yard,
tilting on stiff legs to peck the corncob
clean, to gobble turnip peel, carrot tops, even
the shells of yesterday's eggs. Hens labored
to fill eggboxes the eggman shipped
to Boston, and to provide our breakfast, gathered
at the square table.
                              When the eggmaking frenzy
ceased, when each in her own time set

for weeks as if setting itself made eggs,
each used-up diligent hen
danced on the packed soil of the henyard her final
headless jig, and boiled
in her pale shape featherless as an egg,

                       consumed

like the blind chick, like Nannie
who died one summer at eighty-seven, childish,
deaf, unable to feed herself, demented . . .

Whip-poor-will

Every night about nine
o'clock, when the last light
of June withdraws,
the whip-poor-will sings
his clear brief notes
by the darkening house, then
rises abruptly from sandy
ground, a brown bird
in the near-night, soaring
over shed and woodshed
to far dark fields. When
he returns at dawn,
in my sleep I hear
his three syllables make
a man's name, who slept
fifty years in this bed
and ploughed these fields:
Wes-ley-Wells. . . Wes-
ley-Wells . . .

           It is good
to wake early in high
summer with work to do,

and look out the window
at a ghost bird lifting away
to drowse all morning
in his grassy hut.

A Sister on the Tracks

Between pond and sheepbarn, by maples and watery birches,
Rebecca paces a double line of rust
in a sandy trench, striding on weathered ties,
black creosoted eight-by-eights wedged
into crushed granite.
        The summer of nineteen-forty-three,
long wartrains, skidded tanks,
jeeps, airframes, dynamos, searchlights, and troops
to Montreal for Hitler's War. She counted cars
from the stopped hayrack at the endless crossing:
ninety-nine, one-hundred . . . and her grandfather Ben's
voice shaking with rage and oratory told
how the mighty Boston and Maine
kept the Statehouse in its pocket.
        Today Rebecca walks
a line that vanishes, in solitude
by-passed by wars and commerce. She remembers the story
of the bunting'd day her great-great-great-
grandmother watched the first train roll and smoke
from Potter Place to Gale
with fireworks, cider, and speeches. Then the long rail
drove west, buzzing and humming; the hive of rolling stock
extended a thousand-car'd perspective
from Ohio to Oregon, where men who left stone farms
rode rails toward gold.
        On this blue day she walks

under a high jet's glint of swooped aluminum pulling
its feathery contrail westward. She sees ahead
how the jet dies into junk, and highway wastes
like railroad. Beside her the old creation retires,
hayrack sunk like a rowboat
under its fields of hay. She closes her eyes
to glimpse the vertical track that rises
from the underworld of graves,
soul's ascension connecting dead to unborn. Visionary
rails hum with a hymn of continual vanishing
where tracks cross.
                        For she opens her eyes to read
on a solitary gravestone next to the rails
the familiar names of Ruth and Matthew Bott, born
in a Norfolk parish, who ventured
the immigrant's passionate Exodus westward to labor
on their own land. Here love builds
its mortal house, where today's wind carries
a double scent of heaven and cut hay.

Mr. Wakeville on Interstate 90

"Now I will abandon the route of my life
as my shadowy wives abandon me, taking my children.
I will stop somewhere. I will park in a summer street
where the days tick like metal in the stillness.
Then I will rent the room over Bert's Modern Barbershop
where the TO LET sign leans in the plateglass window;
or I will buy the brown BUNGALOW FOR SALE.

"I will work forty hours a week clerking at the paintstore.
On Fridays I will cash my paycheck at Six Rivers Bank
and stop at Harvey's Market and talk with Harvey.

Walking on Maple Street I will speak to everyone.
At basketball games I will cheer for my neighbors' sons.
I will watch my neighbors' daughters grow up, marry,
raise children. The joints of my fingers will stiffen.

"There will be no room inside me for other places.
I will attend funerals regularly and weddings.
I will chat with the mailman when he comes on Saturdays.
I will shake my head when I hear of the florist
who drops dead in the greenhouse over a flat of pansies;
I spoke with her only yesterday . . .
When lawyer elopes with babysitter I will shake my head.

"When Harvey's boy enlists in the Navy
I will wave goodbye at the Trailways Depot with the others.
I will vote Democratic; I will vote Republican.
I will applaud the valedictorian at graduation
and wish her well as she goes away to the University
and weep as she goes away. I will live in a steady joy;
I will exult in the ecstasy of my concealment."

ANTHONY HECHT

The Book of Yolek

Wir haben ein Gesetz,
Un nach dem Gesetz soll er sterben.

The dowsed coals fume and hiss after your meal
Of grilled brook trout, and you saunter off for a walk
Down the fern trail, it doesn't matter where to,
Just so you're weeks and worlds away from home,
And among midsummer hills have set up camp
In the deep bronze glories of declining day.

You remember, peacefully, an earlier day
In childhood, remember a quite specific meal:
A corn roast and bonfire in summer camp.
That summer you got lost on a "Nature Walk";
More than you dared admit, you thought of home;
No one else knows where the mind wanders to.

The fifth of August, 1942.
It was morning and very hot. It was the day
They came at dawn with rifles to The Home
For Jewish Children, cutting short the meal
Of bread and soup, lining them up to walk
In close formation off to a special camp.

How often you have thought about that camp,
As though in some strange way you were driven to,
And about the children, and how they were made to walk,
Yolek who had bad lungs, who wasn't a day
Over five years old, commanded to leave his meal
And shamble between armed guards to his long home.

We're approaching August again. It will drive home
The regulation torments of that camp
Yolek was sent to, his small, unfinished meal,
The electric fences, the numeral tattoo,
The quite extraordinary heat of the day
They all were forced to take that terrible walk.

Whether on a silent, solitary walk
Or among crowds, far off or safe at home,
You will remember, helplessly, that day,
And the smell of smoke, and the loudspeakers of the camp.
Wherever you are, Yolek will be there, too.
His unuttered name will interrupt your meal.

Prepare to receive him in your home some day.
Though they killed him in the camp they sent him to,
He will walk in as you're sitting down to a meal.

The Transparent Man

I'm mighty glad to see you, Mrs. Curtis,
And thank you very kindly for this visit—
Especially now when all the others here
Are having holiday visitors, and I feel
A little conspicuous and in the way.
It's mainly because of Thanksgiving. All these mothers
And wives and husbands gaze at me soulfully
And feel they should break up their box of chocolates
For a donation, or hand me a chunk of fruitcake.
What they don't understand and never guess
Is that it's better for me without a family;
It's a great blessing. Though I mean no harm.
And as for visitors, why, I have you,
All cheerful, brisk and punctual every Sunday,

Like church, even if the aisles smell of phenol.
And you always bring even better gifts than any
On your book-trolley. Though they mean only good,
Families can become a sort of burden.
I've only got my father, and he won't come,
Poor man, because it would be too much for him.
And for me, too, so it's best the way it is.
He knows, you see, that I will predecease him,
Which is hard enough. It would take a callous man
To come and stand around and watch me failing.
(Now don't you fuss; we both know the plain facts.)
But for him it's even harder. He loved my mother.
They say she looked like me; I suppose she may have.
Or rather, as I grew older I came to look
More and more like she must one time have looked,
And so the prospect for my father now
Of losing me is like having to lose her twice.
I know he frets about me. Dr. Frazer
Tells me he phones in every single day,
Hoping that things will take a turn for the better.
But with leukemia things don't improve.
It's like a sort of blizzard in the bloodstream,
A deep, severe, unseasonable winter,
Burying everything. The white blood cells
Multiply crazily and storm around,
Out of control. The chemotherapy
Hasn't helped much, and it makes my hair fall out.
I know I look a sight, but I don't care.
I care about fewer things; I'm more selective.
It's got so I can't even bring myself
To read through any of your books these days.
It's partly weariness, and partly the fact
That I seem not to care much about the endings,
How things work out, or whether they even do.
What I do instead is sit here by this window

And look out at the trees across the way.
You wouldn't think that was much, but let me tell you,
It keeps me quite intent and occupied.
Now all the leaves are down, you can see the spare,
Delicate structures of the sycamores,
The fine articulation of the beeches.
I have sat here for days studying them,
And I have only just begun to see
What it is that they resemble. One by one,
They stand there like magnificent enlargements
Of the vascular system of the human brain.
I see them there like huge discarnate minds,
Lost in their meditative silences.
The trunks, branches and twigs compose the vessels
That feed and nourish vast immortal thoughts.
So I've assigned them names. There, near the path,
Is the great brain of Beethoven, and Kepler
Haunts the wide spaces of that mountain ash.
This view, you see, has become my Hall of Fame.
It came to me one day when I remembered
Mary Beth Finley who used to play with me
When we were girls. One year her parents gave her
A birthday toy called "The Transparent Man."
It was made of plastic, with different colored organs,
And the circulatory system all mapped out
In rivers of red and blue. She'd ask me over
And the two of us would sit and study him
Together, and do a powerful lot of giggling.
I figure he's most likely the only man
Either of us would ever get to know
Intimately, because Mary Beth became
A Sister of Mercy when she was old enough.
She must be thirty-one; she was a year
Older than I, and about four inches taller.
I used to envy both those advantages

Back in those days. Anyway, I was struck
Right from the start by the sea-weed intricacy,
The fine-haired, silken-threaded filiations
That wove, like Belgian lace, throughout the head.
But this last week it seems I have found myself
Looking beyond, or through, individual trees
At the dense, clustered woodland just behind them,
Where those great, nameless crowds patiently stand.
It's become a sort of complex, ultimate puzzle
And keeps me fascinated. My eyes are twenty-twenty,
Or used to be, but of course I can't unravel
The tousled snarl of intersecting limbs,
That mackled, cinder grayness. It's a riddle
Beyond the eye's solution. Impenetrable.
If there is order in all that anarchy
Of granite mezzotint, that wilderness,
It takes a better eye than mine to see it.
It set me on to wondering how to deal
With such a thickness of particulars,
Deal with it faithfully, you understand,
Without blurring the issue. Of course I know
That within a month the sleeving snows will come
With cold, selective emphases, with massings
And arbitrary contrasts, rendering things
Deceptively simple, thickening the twigs
To frosty veins, bestowing epaulets
And decorations on every birch and aspen.
And the eye, self-satisfied, will be misled,
Thinking the puzzle solved, supposing at last
It can look forth and comprehend the world.
That's when you have to really watch yourself.
So I hope that you won't think me plain ungrateful
For not selecting one of your fine books,
And I take it very kindly that you came
And sat here and let me rattle on this way.

Meditation

For William Alfred

I

The orchestra tunes up, each instrument
In lunatic monologue putting on its airs,
Oblivious, haughty, full of self-regard.
The flute fingers its priceless strand of pearls,
Nasal disdain is eructed by the horn,
The strings let drop thin overtones of malice,
Inchoate, like the dense *rhubarb* of voices
At a cocktail party, which the ear sorts out
By alert exclusions, keen selectivities.
A five-way conversation, at its start
Smooth and intelligible as a Brahms quintet,
Disintegrates after one's third martini
To dull orchestral nonsense, the garbled fragments
Of domestic friction in a foreign tongue,
Accompanied by a private sense of panic:
This surely must be how old age arrives,
Quite unannounced, when suddenly one fine day
Some trusted faculty has gone forever.

II

After the closing of cathedral doors,
After the last soft footfall fades away,
There still remain artesian, grottoed sounds
Below the threshold of the audible,
Those infinite, unspent reverberations
Of the prayers, coughs, whispers and *amens* of the day,
Afloat upon the marble surfaces.
They continue forever. Nothing is ever lost.
So the shouts of children, enriched, magnifed,
Cross-fertilized by the contours of a tunnel,

Promote their little statures for a moment
Of resonance to authority and notice,
A fleeting, bold celebrity that rounds
In perfect circles to attentive shores,
Returning now in still enlarging arcs
To which there is no end. Whirled without end.

III

This perfect company is here engaged
In what is called a sacred conversation.
A seat has been provided for the lady
With her undiapered child in a bright loggia
Floored with *antico verde* and alabaster
Which are cool and pleasing to the feet of saints
Who stand at either side. It is eight o'clock
On a sunny April morning, and there is much here
Worthy of observation. First of all,
No one in all the group seems to be speaking.
The Baptist, in a rude garment of hides,
Vaguely unkempt, is looking straight at the viewer
With serious interest, patient and unblinking.
Across from him, relaxed but powerful,
Stands St. Sebastian, who is neither a ruse
To get a young male nude with classic torso
Into an obviously religious painting,
Nor one who suffers his target martyrdom
Languidly or with a masochist's satisfaction.
He experiences a kind of acupuncture
That in its blessedness has set him free
To attend to everything except himself.
Jerome and Francis, the one in his red hat,
The other tonsured, both of them utterly silent,
Cast their eyes downward as in deep reflection.
Perched on a marble dais below the lady
A small seraphic consort of viols and lutes

Prepares to play or actually is playing.
They exhibit furrowed, child-like concentration.
A landscape of extraordinary beauty
Leads out behind the personages to where
A shepherd tends his flock. Far off a ship
Sets sail for the world of commerce. Travelers
Kneel at a wayside shrine near a stone wall.
Game-brids or song-birds strut or take the air
In gliding vectors among cypress spires
By contoured vineyards or groves of olive trees.
A belfry crowns a little knoll behind which
The world recedes into a cobalt blue
Horizon of remote, fine mountain peaks.

    The company, though they have turned their backs
To all of this, are aware of everything.
Beneath their words, but audible, the silver
Liquidities of stream and song-bird fall
In cleansing passages, and the water-wheel
Turns out its measured, periodic creak.
They hear the coughs, the raised voices of children
Joyful in the dark tunnel, everything.
Observe with care their tranquil pensiveness.
They hear all the petitions, all the cries
Reverberating over marble floors,
Floating above still water in dark wells.
All the world's woes, all the world's woven woes,
The warp of ages, they hear and understand,
To which is added a final bitterness:
That their own torments, deaths, renunciations,
Made in the name of love, have served as warrant,
Serve to this very morning as fresh warrant
For the infliction of new atrocities.
All this they know. Nothing is ever lost.
It is the condition of their blessedness

To hear and recall the recurrent cries of pain
And parse them into a discourse that consorts
In strange agreement with the viols and lutes,
Which, with the water and the meadow bells,
And every gathered voice, every *amen*,
Join to compose the sacred conversation.

Murmur

Look in thy heart and write.
—SIDNEY
O heart, O troubled heart—
—YEATS

A little sibilance, as of dry leaves,
Or dim, sibylline whisper, not quite heard:
Thus famously the powers that be converse
Just out of earshot, and theirs is the last word.
Officiously they mutter about our lives.
The die is cast, they say. *For better or worse.*

Thus the Joint Chiefs. Thus, too, the Underground.
Soft susurrations reach us where we repose
On a porch at evening. We notice a vague uproar
Of bees in the hollyhocks. Does the darkening rose
Hum with an almost imperceptible sound?
That small vibrato, is it news of a distant war?

You've seen the night nurse, who hugs your fever chart
Defensively to her bosom's alpine slopes,
Confer with an interne who lounges against a wall,
A boy not half your age. They converse apart.
And nothing they say seems to provoke a smile
As they stand there earnestly trifling with your hopes.

And remember again the long-distance telephone
When you're asked to hold the line, and way far off
A woman's crack-voiced, broken-hearted plea
Is answered only by a toneless cough.
You have stumbled upon some gross fatality
There in the void—quite possibly your own.

This latest leak from an invisible source
Speaks like the slave appointed to hover near
The emperor, triumph-crowned in gold and myrtle,
And regularly to breathe in Caesar's ear
As they pursue the *via sacra's* course
Through the great crowds, "Remember you are mortal."

MARK JARMAN

Le Touquet

If we could miss a ship every day
And return every day to le Touquet
And run the film of the tidal flats
With the tide far out and a mist of gnats
Dancing like us, the film's tattoo
Flexing comically to make us go
In a wriggle across the colorless sand,
If we could draw from an empty hand
All that sweetness of the past together
—But Father no longer loves Mother.

Grown children, watching a film strip sharpen
Grief, know that anything can happen.
Missing a ride to the cliffs of Dover
One summer, a summer played over and over,
Made a mishap into a glory.
The record shows nobody sorry.
Father would shoot, then Mother would shoot.
And the pictures, though of course they date
The young parents, prove what I say
—They were happy at le Touquet.

In Hell

The anteroom was just a modern lobby
Tiled with blue, cast earthenware and hung
With seascapes. The tiles (I peered at their detail)

Climbed the walls, too. I approached a lady
Seated primly as a white chrysanthemum
At her bare desk. A bit long in tooth and nail,

But businesslike, she smiled, directing me
Three doors and one floor down. My bare soles
Felt warm, but I jumped to no conclusions
And padded down the hall, almost free,
It seemed, almost free. And even though
I had to go back twice to ask directions,

Nothing changed in her downy, hard demeanor,
A soft explosion as right as it was wrong.
When finally I found my way, I stopped
Before a suite of rooms that didn't square
With where it was. The shock was sure and strong.
Women were giving birth here. Urged and helped,

They opened completely to the giving-up.
The babies slid from underneath the green
Of hospital drapes, squalling, and were bedded
On stainless steel. Doctors' hands were cupped
To catch them. A busy place where all were fine—
Mothers and children. Nothing was regretted.

But after that, nothing was so odd.
I found my door, and the glimmer of a joke
From seventh grade about the doors of hell
Unsettled my ease that things were not so bad,
That agony might be a piece of cake
Since it had to end. Then, down the stairwell,

I followed a channel of water suddenly
Descending the salmon ladder of the stairs.
A kind of flesh, the water crawled beside me,

And at my floor (the one-down she had told me),
It snaked, a gray skin, among the chairs,
Through rooms I'd lived in with my family.

Hacking at the skein with bailing pails
Were arms and hands. Levers and frantic gears
Of sweaty engines, machines of human flesh,
Churned at every angle. I could not feel
Pain, I was sure. And then I saw the smears,
Flecks, spots on everything, like slaughtered flies.

The reek came off of years of memory:
Off couches angled for loving, idle talk;
Clocks set to warm the night with bonging brass;
Plates clutched in wire crabs; crockery
Hoarded up in hutches. The odor balked
Breath. And, butchered as it went, the water passed.

So, this was it. The plunging buckets spun
The stream of useless fluid to light froth
That clung like mist, leaving a porous film.
So, here it was. I nearly called it home,
But I was wrong again. The channel's mouth
Funneled outside to a fountain, a burst of fun.

There, grinning through the fountain's screen of spray,
Human and animal shapes carved from stone
Came to life as kids and family pets,
Splashing one another. As I stood by,
I saw others who thought they were alone
Watching this happen, wondering what was next,

If we could join. But tilting into view,
At first like dawn, then like a nighttime flank
Of mountain range on fire, a black and red

Something (the place itself?) cracked and drew
Down laughter, water, light, and so we sank—
Or rather, walked on quickly. Just ahead,

I saw a group I knew—my mother, sisters,
My father, too. I fell in step with them.
The tunnel we went into broadcast words
About its length and darkness. Then the strangers
Crowded close behind—I couldn't stop them—
And we, just bodies now, kept pressing forwards.

Clues to Displaced Persons

I

The old, heavy, engraved tabletop caught crumbs
She ran out with a fingernail, then she ran out of air.
On both splayed hands, as big as her husband's,
She found rest and breath looking out at the garden.
It was noon. The frogs were sleeping
Or darting like retorts you keep to yourself
Deep under the pond lid, in the flabby serenity.
The windows, at least, let her out into the world,
Already rubbed clean, clear to the redwood's shadow.
It is easy to believe she is ashes now,
And the ashes, poured in a file box, hold their breath
Behind the brick of a fountain. Easy to believe
This big woman who blew a sliding whistle
To call her son home is out of reach.

2

Big as her husband's hands, but his were dainty,
Featureless, like blocks for gloves, but hands—
And with them he signed her over to the mortuary,

The crematorium, and offered her ashes
To the mason cutting curls of ripe mortar.
He went on wearing his clerical vestments,
The doctor's bars and the Hallowe'en colored hood.
Where is he? His son buried him in the robes,
The hood, the reputation, ordered the stone
With only the surname, and made the last payment.
His slab lay flush with the grass. Where is he?
The park went into decline, if you can believe it—
A graveyard bankrupt. We have the map of plots,
And guesses as good as gravel tossed in the air.

                              3
I have not heard from you, it seems, in a year.
Your mother and father, Father, both are buried—
Lost beyond death, in fact, better than dead.
I have not heard. But what do I want to hear?
That there is a clue to find you in one piece,
One place, having been freed, having freed yourself
Of all of us, the dead and the living, too?
Mother drank a bottle of Romanian wine
And cursed your stupid closing of the past.
Then you called, and she blew you a bubble of laughter.
If I could climb her love, like the redwood
In your mother's yard to that crow's-nest of sunlight
Where I could just see the Pacific,
Would I see you? Where did you call from?

ERICA JONG

In the Glass-Bottomed Boat

In the glass-bottomed boat
of our lives, we putter along
gazing at that other world
under the sea—
that world of flickering
yellow-tailed fish,
of deadly moray eels, of sea urchins
like black stars
that devastate great brains
of coral,
of fish the color
of blue neon,
& fish the color
liquid silver
made by Indians
exterminated
centuries ago.

We pass, we pass,
always looking down.
The fish do not
look up at us,
as if they knew
somehow
their world
for the eternal one,
ours for
the merely time-bound.

The engine sputters.
Our guide—a sweet
black boy with skin
the color of molten chocolate—
asks us of the price of jeans
& karate classes,
in the States.
Surfboards too
delight him—
& skateboards.
He wants to sail, sail, sail
not putter
through the world.

& so do we,
so do we,
wishing for the freedom
of the fish
beneath the reef,
wishing for the crevices
of sunken ship
with its rusted eye-holes,
its great ribbed hull,
its rotted rudder,
its bright propeller
tarnishing beneath the sea.

"They sunk this ship
on purpose,"
says our guide—
which does not surprise
us,
knowing how life
always imitates

even the shabbiest
art.
Our brains forged
in shark & sea-wreck epics,
we fully expect to see
a wreck like this one,
made on purpose
for our eyes.

But the fish swim on,
intimating death,
intimating outer space,
& even the oceans
within the body
from which we come.

The fish are uninterested
in us.
What hubris to think
a shark concentrates
as much on us
as we on him!

the creatures of the reef
spell death, spell life,
spell eternity,
& still we putter on
in our leaky little boat,
halfway there,
halfway there.

DONALD JUSTICE

Complaint of the Grandparents

Les morts
C'est sous terre;
Ça n'en sort
Guère.
— LAFORGUE

Our diaries squatted, toad-like,
On dark closet ledges.
Forget-me-not and thistle
Decalcomaned the pages.
But where, where are they now,
    All the sad squalors
    Of those between-wars parlors?—
Wax fruit; and the sunlight spilt like soda
    On torporous rugs; the photo
    Albums all outspread . . .
        The dead
Don't get around much anymore.

There was an hour when daughters
Practiced arpeggios.
Their mothers, awkward and proud,
Would listen, smoothing their hose.
Sundays, half-past five!
    Do you recall
    How the sun used to loll,
Lazily, just beyond the roof,
    Bloodshot and aloof?
    We thought it would never set.
       The dead don't get
Around much anymore.

Eternity resembles
One long Sunday afternoon.
No traffic passes; the cigar-smoke
Coils in a blue cocoon.
Children, have you nothing
    For our cold sakes?
No tea? No little tea-cakes?
Sometimes now the rains disturb
    Even our remote suburb.
There's a dampness underground . . .
    The dead don't get around
    Much anymore.

Variations on Southern Themes

I. AT THE CEMETERY

But why do I write of the all unutterable and
the all abysmal? Why does my pen not drop from
my hand on approaching the infinite pity and
tragedy of all the past? It does, poor helpless
pen, with what it meets of the ineffable, what it
meets of the cold Medusa-face of life, of all the
life lived, on every side. Basta, basta!
    —HENRY JAMES, *Notebooks*

Above the fence-flowers, like a bloody thumb,
A hummingbird is throbbing, throbbing. Some
Petals take motion now from the beaten wings
In hardly observable obscure quiverings.
And mother stands there, but so still her clothing
Seems to have settled into stone, nothing
To animate her face, nothing to read there—
O plastic rose O clouds O still cedar!
And she stands there a long time while the sky
Ponders her with its great Medusa-eye;

Or in my memory she does. And then a
Slow blacksnake, lazy with long sunning, glides
Down from its slab, and through the thick grass, and hides
Somewhere among the purpling wild verbena.

2. ON THE FARM

And I, missing the city intensely at this moment,
Mope and sulk at the window. There's the first owl now, quite near,
But the sound hardly registers. And the kerosene lamp
Goes on sputtering, giving off vague medicinal fumes
That make me think of sick-rooms. I have been memorizing
'The Ballad of Reading Gaol,' but the lamplight hurts my eyes.
And I am too bored to sleep, restless and bored. I think of
The city . . .
                    As, years later, I will recall, without blame,
The tender banalities of those dead Julys—but, ah,
The bitterness of the lampsmoke still, the pure aloneness!
Soon now I yawn, and the old dream of being a changeling
Returns. I hear the owl, and I think myself like the owl—
Proud, almost unnoticed—or like some hero in Homer
Protected by a cloud let down by the gods to save me.

3. IN THE TRAIN, HEADING NORTH THROUGH FLORIDA, LATE AT NIGHT AND LONG AGO, AND ENDING WITH A LINE FROM THOMAS WOLFE

Midnight or after, and the little lights
Glitter like lost beads from a broken necklace
Beyond smudged windows, lost and irretrievable—
Some promise of romance these Southern nights
Never entirely keep—unless, sleepless,
We should pass down dim corridors again
To stand, braced in a swaying vestibule,
Alone with the darkness and the wind—out there
Nothing but pines and one new road perhaps,
Straight and white, aimed at the distant gulf—

And hear, from the smoking-room, the sudden high-pitched
Whinny of laughter pass from throat to throat;
And the great wheels smash and pound beneath our feet.

Tremayne

1. THE MILD DESPAIR OF TREMAYNE

Snow melting and the dog
Barks lonely on his bottom from the yard.
The ground is frozen but not hard.

The seasonal and vague
Despairs of February settle over
Tremayne now like a light snow cover,

And he sits thinking; sits
Also not thinking for a while of much.
So February turns to March.

Snow turns to rain; a hyacinth
Pokes up; doves returning moan and sing.
Tremayne takes note of one more spring—

Mordancies of the armchair!—
And finds it hard not to be reconciled
To a despair that seems so mild.

2. THE CONTENTMENT OF TREMAYNE

Tremayne stands in the sunlight,
Watering his lawn.
The sun seems not to move at all,
Till it has moved on.

The twilight sounds commence then,
 As those of water cease,
And he goes barefoot through the stir,
 Almost at peace.

Light leans in pale rectangles
 Out against the night.
Tremayne asks nothing more now. There's
 Just enough light,

Or when the street lamp catches
 There should be. He pauses:
How simple it all seems for once!—
 These sidewalks, these still houses.

3. THE INSOMNIA OF TREMAYNE

The all-night stations—Tremayne pictures them
As towers shooting great sparks through the dark—
Fade out and drift among the drifted hours
Just now returning to his bedside clock;
And something starts all over, call it day.
He likes, he really likes the little hum,
Which is the last sound of all night-sounds to decay.

Call this the static of the spheres, a sound
Of pure in-betweenness, far, and choked, and thin.
As long as it lasts—a faint, celestial surf—
He feels no need to dial the weather in,
Or music, or the news, or anything.
And it soothes him, like some night-murmuring nurse,
Murmuring nothing much, perhaps, but murmuring.

4. TREMAYNE AUTUMNAL

Autumn, and a cold rain, and mist,
In which the dark pine-shapes are drowned,

And taller pole-shapes, and the town lights masked—
A scene, oh, vaguely Post-Impressionist,
  Tremayne would tell us, if we asked.

  Who with his glasses off, half blind,
  Accomplishes very much the same
Lovely effect of blurs and shimmerings—
Or else October evenings spill a kind
  Of Lethe-water over things.

  "O season of half forgetfulness!"
  Tremayne, as usual, misquotes,
Recalling adolescence and old trees
In whose shade once he memorized that verse
  And something about "late flowers for the bees . . ."

October

Summer, goodbye.
The days grow shorter.
Cranes walk the fairway now
In careless order.

They step so gradually
Toward the distant green
They might be brushstrokes
Animating a screen.

Mist canopies
The water hazard.
Nearby, the little flag lifts,
Brave but frazzled.

Under sad clouds
Two white-capped golfers
Stand looking off, dreamy and strange,
Like young girls in Balthus.

Villanelle at Sundown

Turn your head, look, the light is turning yellow.
The river seems enriched thereby, not to say deepened.
Why this is I'll never be able to tell you.

Or are Americans half in love with failure?
One used to say so, reading in Fitzgerald, as it happened.
(Our Viking Portable, all water-spotted and yellow,

Remember?) Or does mere distance lend this value
To things?—false, it may be, but the view is hardly cheapened.
Why this is I'll never be able to tell you.

The smoke, those tiny cars, the whole urban milieu—
One can like *any*thing diminishment has sharpened.
Our painter friend, Lang, might show the whole thing yellow

And not be much off. It's nuance that counts, not color—
As in some late James novel, saved up for a long weekend,
And vivid with all the master simply won't tell you.

How frail our generation has got, how sallow
And pinched with just surviving! We all go off the deep end
Finally, gold beaten thinly out to yellow,
And why this is I'll never be able to tell you.

X. J. KENNEDY

Abyss

from Charles Baudelaire

Wherever Pascal went, went his abyss,
    That good dog. All's one chasm now: wish, word,
    Dream, deed. Over my hair that when it's scared
Rears upright on its roots, I feel wind cross.

Up, down, around me—fathomlessness, loss,
    Silence, seductive space. On night's black board
    The professorial finger of the Lord
Traces unending nightmares, and I toss,

Leery of sleep as of some gaping pit
    Oozing with spooks, that leads down who knows where.
My every window frames an Infinite,

Vertigo shrieks inside me, and my soul's
    Jealous of voids—at least, they're unaware.
Christ! stuck for life with beings! numerals!

Pont Mirabeau

from Guillaume Apollinare

Underneath Pont Mirabeau flows the Seine
    And loves of ours
    Must I remember back when
Joy followed always in the wake of pain

        Evening come   be sounded hour
        The days go running   I stand here

Hands in my hands stay with me face to face
    While underneath
    The bridge of our embrace
Of everlasting gazes tired the wave passes

        Evening come   be sounded hour
        The days go running   I stand here

Love goes on by as running water went
    Love goes on by
    As life is   indolent
And hope of happiness is   violent

        Evening come   be sounded hour
        The days go running   I stand here

Though the days pass and passing weeks run on
    No time gone by
    Nor love comes back again
Underneath Pont Mirabeau flows the Seine

        Evening come   be sounded hour
        The days go running   I stand here

Ambition

First blow of October. Now oak leaves shy
Down from branches they value not overly high
As though to let go and abandon stem
Or to stay growing old didn't matter to them.

I'd be glad to go out on a limb with those
Who want nothing beyond what the wind bestows,
Were I not bound to roots, dug in deep to bear
Never being done grasping for light and air.

GALWAY KINNELL

The Fundamental Project of Technology

A flash! A white flash sparkled!
—TATSUICHIRO AKIZUKI,
Concentric Circles of Death

Under glass: glass dishes which changed
in color; pieces of transformed beer bottles;
a household iron; bundles of wire become solid
lumps of iron; a pair of pliers; a ring of skull-
bone fused to the inside of a helmet; a pair of eyeglasses
taken off the eyes of an eyewitness, without glass,
which vanished, when a white flash sparkled.

An old man, possibly a soldier back then,
now reduced down to one who soon will die,
sucks at the cigaret dangling from his lip, peers
at the uniform, scorched, of some tiniest schoolboy,
sighs out bluish mists of his own ashes over
a pressed tin lunch box well crushed back then when
the word *future* first learned, in a white flash, to jerk tears.

On the bridge outside, in navy black, a group
of schoolchildren line up, hold it, grin at a flash-pop,
scatter like pigeons across grass, see a stranger, cry,
hello! hello! hello! and soon *goodbye! goodbye! goodbye!*
having pecked up the greetings that fell half unspoken
and the going-sayings that those who went the day
it happened a white flash sparkled did not get to say.

If all a city's faces were to shrink back all at once
from their skulls, would a new sound came into existence,
audible above moans eaves extract from wind that smoothes
the grass on graves or raspings heart's-blood greases still
or wails infants trill born already skillful at the grandpa's rattle
or infra-screams bitter-knowledge's speechlessness
memorized, at that white flash, inside closed-forever mouths?

To de-animalize human mentality, to purge it of obsolete
evolutionary characteristics, in particular of death,
which foreknowledge terrorizes the contents of skulls with,
is the fundamental project of technology; however,
pseudologica fantastica's mechanisms require:
to establish deathlessness it is necessary first to eliminate
those who die; a task attempted, when a white flash sparkled.

Unlike the trees of home, which continually evaporate
along the skyline, the trees here have been enticed down
toward world-eternity. No one knows which gods they enshrine.
Does it matter? Awareness of ignorance is as devout
as knowledge of knowledge. Or more so. Even though not knowing,
sometimes we weep, from surplus of gratitude, even though knowing,
twice already on earth sparkled a flash, a white flash.

The children go away. By nature they do. And by memory,
in scorched uniforms, holding tiny crushed lunch tins.
All the ecstasy-groans of each night call them back, satori
their ghostliness back into the ashes, in the momentary shrines,
the thankfulness of arms, from which they will go
again and again, until the day flashes and no one lives
to look back and say, a flash, a white flash sparkled.

MAXINE KUMIN

Shelling Jacobs Cattle Beans

All summer
they grew unseen
in the corn patch
planted to climb on Silver Queen
Butter and Sugar
compete with witch
grass and lamb's-quarters
only to stand naked, old crones,
Mayan, Macedonian
sticks of antiquity
drying alone
after the corn is taken.

I, whose ancestors
put on sackcloth and ashes
for the destruction of the Temple
sit winnowing the beans
on Rosh Hashonah
in the September sun
of New Hampshire.
Each its own example:
a rare bird's egg
cranberry- or blood-flecked
as cool in the hand
as a beach stone
no two exactly alike
yet close as snowflakes.
Each pops out of the dry

husk, the oblong shaft
that held it,
every compartment a tight fit.

I sit on the front stoop
a romantic, thinking
what a centerpiece!
not, what a soup!
layering beans into
their storage jars.
At Pompeii the food
ossified on the table
under strata of ash.
Before that, the Hebrews
stacked bricks
under the Egyptian lash.

Today
in the slums of Lebanon
Semite is set against Semite
with Old Testament fervor.
Bombs go off in Paris,
Damascus, New York,
a network of retaliations.
Where is the God of
my fathers, that I

may pluck Him out of the lineup?
That I may hand back my ticket?

In case we outlast
the winter, in case
when the end comes
ending all matter,

the least gravel
of Jacobs Cattle remain,
let me shell out the lot.
Let me put my faith in the bean.

Grandchild

For Yann

All night the *douanier* in his sentry box
at the end of the lane where France begins plays fox
and hounds with little spurts of cars
that sniff to a stop at the barrier
and declare themselves. I stand at the window
watching the ancient boundaries that flow
between my daughter's life and mine dissolve
like taffy pulled until it melts in half
without announcing any point of strain
and I am a young unsure mother again
stiffly clutching the twelve-limbed raw
creature that broke from between my legs, that stew
of bone and membrane loosely sewn up in
a fierce scared flailing other being.

We blink, two strangers in a foreign kitchen.
Now that you've drained your mother dry and will
not sleep, I take you in my arms, brimful
six days old, little feared-for mouse.
Last week when you were still a fish
in the interior, I dreamed you thus:
The *douanier* brought you curled up in his cap
buttoned and suited like him, authority's prop
—a good Victorian child's myth—

and in his other hand a large round cheese
ready to the point of runniness.
At least there, says the dream, no mysteries.

Toward dawn I open my daughter's cupboard on
a choice of calming teas—*infusions*—
verbena, fennel, linden, camomile,
shift you on my shoulder and fill the kettle.
Age has conferred on me a certain grace.
You're a package I can rock and ease
from wakefulness to sleep. This skill comes back
like learning how to swim. Comes warm and quick
as first milk in the breasts. I comfort you.
Body to body my monkey-wit soaks through.

Later, I wind the outside shutters up.
You sleep mouse-mild, topped with camomile.
Daylight slips past the *douane*. I rinse my cup.
My daughter troubles sleep a little while
longer. The just-milked cows across the way
come down their hillside single file
and the dream, the lefthand gift of ripened brie
recurs, smelly, natural, and good
wanting only to be brought true
in your own time: your childhood.

STANLEY KUNITZ

The Abduction

Some things I do not profess
to understand, perhaps
not wanting to, including
whatever it was they did
with you or you with them
that timeless summer day
when you stumbled out of the wood,
distracted, with your white blouse torn
and a bloodstain on your skirt.
"Do you believe?" you asked.
Between us, through the years,
from bits, from broken clues,
we pieced enough together
to make the story real:
how you encountered on the path
a pack of sleek, grey hounds,
trailed by a dumbshow retinue
in leather shrouds; and how
you were led, through leafy ways,
into the presence of a royal stag,
flaming in his chestnut coat,
who kneeled on a swale of moss
before you; and how you were borne
aloft in triumph through the green,
stretched on his rack of budding horn,
till suddenly you found yourself alone
in a trampled clearing.

That was a long time ago,
almost another age, but even now,
when I hold you in my arms,
I wonder where you are.
Sometimes I wake to hear
the engines of the night thrumming
outside the east bay window
on the lawn spreading to the rose garden.
You lie beside me in elegant repose,
a hint of transport hovering on your lips,
indifferent to the harsh green flares
that swivel through the room,
searchlights controlled by unseen hands.
Out there is childhood country,
bleached faces peering in
with coals for eyes.
Our lives are spinning out
from world to world;
the shapes of things
are shifting in the wind.
What do we know
beyond the rapture and the dread?

The Long Boat

When his boat snapped loose
from its moorings, under
the screaking of the gulls,
he tried at first to wave
to his dear ones on shore,
but in the rolling fog
they had already lost their faces.
Too tired even to choose

between jumping and calling,
somehow he felt absolved and free
of his burdens, those mottoes
stamped on his name-tag:
conscience, ambition, and all
that caring.
He was content to lie down
with the family ghosts
in the slop of his cradle,
buffeted by the storm,
endlessly drifting.
Peace! Peace!
To be rocked by the Infinite!
As if it didn't matter
which way was home;
as if he didn't know
he loved the earth so much
he wanted to stay forever.

Lamplighter: 1914

What I remember most was not
the incident at Sarajevo,
but the first flying steamkettle
puffing round the bend,
churning up the dirt
between the rocky pastures
as it came riding high
on its red wheels
in a blare of shining brass;
and my bay stallion snorting,
rearing in fright, bolting,
leaving me sprawled on the ground;

and our buggy
careening out of sight,
those loose reins dangling,
racing toward its rendezvous
with Hammond's stone wall
in an explosion of wood and flesh,
the crack of smashed cannon bones.
Who are these strangers
sprung out of the fields?
It is my friend, almost my brother,
who points a gun
to the crooked head.

Once I was a lamplighter
on the Quinnapoxet roads,
making the rounds with Prince,
who was older than I and knew
by heart each of our stations,
needing no whoa of command
nor a tug at his bridle.
That was the summer I practiced
sleight-of-hand and fell asleep
over my picture-books of magic.
Toward dusk, at crossings
and at farmhouse gates,
under the solitary iron trees
I stood on the rim of the buggy wheel
and raised my enchanter's wand,
with its tip of orange flame,
to the gas mantles in their cages,
touching them, one by one,
till the whole countryside bloomed.

The Snakes of September

All summer I heard them
rustling in the shrubbery,
outracing me from tier
to tier in my garden,
a whisper among the viburnums,
a signal flashed from the hedgerow,
a shadow pulsing
in the barberry thicket.
Now that the nights are chill
and the annuals spent,
I should have thought them gone,
in a torpor of blood
slipped to the nether world
before the sickle frost.
Not so. In the deceptive balm
of noon, as if defiant of the curse
that spoiled another garden,
these two appear on show
through a narrow slit
in the dense green brocade
of a north-country spruce,
dangling head-down, entwined
in a brazen love-knot.
I put out my hand and stroke
the fine, dry grit of their skins.
After all,
we are partners in this land,
co-signers of a covenant.
At my touch the wild
braid of creation
trembles.

SYDNEY LEA

After Labor Day

Your son is seven years dead.
"But it seems," I said, seeing your face
buckle in mid-conversation
as over the fields came winging the trebles
of children at holiday play—
I said, "But it seems like yesterday."

"No," you said,
"Like today."

In the first of the black fall drizzles,
in a morning when world's-end seems to hover
too near, the early fallen
leaves slick on the highway as blood,
the yellow ball had spun to a halt
on the white line:
your small child scurried there like an ignorant vole . . .

It is the time of year
when hawks rush down the pass where you live,
but the heat last weekend held them
northward. So grounded, we talked like voluble schoolkids
inside, instead. —Or I did.
You lost in thought, dark brows arched
like the wings of birds at travel,
or soaring to hide, or seek.

At home, I recall your eagle visage, how now
and then it falls
just so. In the change, in the first cold autumn rain,

I play at identification.
I imagine how Redtail, Cooper's,
Roughleg, Little Blue Darter,
and the odd outsider—Swainson's, say—
now pass you by,
as at home in my study I watch
two scruffy starlings on a wire outside
fronting what they seem to have
no choice but to front
till one peels off, is sucked it seems into woods, and through
the glass I yet can hear him.
His croaks come this way, as if the other
were the one who had vanished, not he.

Just so lost children imagine
their parents are lost, not they.
"Where did you go?" they chirp, as if we hadn't been
shrieking, searching.
Or as if our terror had been a game.

It's the season of the mushroom all of a sudden.

Closed though my window is,
over the vapors and trees I also hear
the doubled scream of a kestrel.

You heard, these seven years have heard, the swish
of tandem tires through puddles,
the last gasps
of airbrakes, screams.
And loud as unthinkable detonation
—or so at least in dreams it seems—
the impact:

every outside sound raced clear to you.
But walls and panes cut short your shouts
from inside the house,
as if *you* were the small boy
to whom the remote roar
of the world was suddenly apparent,
yet whose voice was as in dreams
unheard or worse: irrelevant.

In the lulls, by way of compensation,
I talked the holiday away.
Talked and talked and
talked and talked
and catalogued the game:
I called attention
to early Goldeneyes out on the marsh;
to the way in later light
—like cheap raincoats—the feather's colors
on the backs of seaducks would change and change;
and, higher, to the cloud that would mean this greater change,
swooping against the yellow ball of the sun.

As if through a shield of thin glass,
there was the further drone of the bomber whereby,
you said, "One day the world will be lost,"

and the bitter joke, I understood,
be on those of us who all these seasons
have played at discourse.
"Where did you go?"
So the world will ask.

Sereno

—5 December 1982

Month when my cord to the womb was cut, yet almost hot
this wind, all strung with ducks, with Oldsquaw, Bufflehead
and Whistler. And the ones I'm after—high,

The clever Blacks, who stretch their necks, and circle, and light
out of my range for good. There was a time
this might have prompted anger, and anger self-contempt:

What was I doing here, blue feet and fingers blocks like wood,
the very moisture of my eyes iced over, and icebergs in my blood?
My blood flows easier with age, the rage to question

Faltering. Like useless thoughts, the trash-birds strafe my blind.
My poor dogs whine: why does the gun stay silent?
Because, as I can't tell them—because I simply watch

The nobler ducks catch whiteness off the sun,
which grows these days each day more rare,
and the bay's best blue. Parade of change.

The wind from north is warm, is wafting
forgiveness here. To noble and ignoble.
Here on Frenchman's Cove on a spit of land, and blinded,

In this strangely torpid season I forgive
the bullies and the bullied, everyone and -thing
who wants to live, that wants to live,

The chasers and the chased:
the killer put to death today by pentathol injection,
Charlie Brooks in Texas;

I forgive the injectors;
I forgive the intractable shyness of all secrets,
like the ducks that stay far out of range.

I forgive all beings in their desperation:
murdered, murderer; mothers, fathers wanting something
the children they bring forth can't give;

Myself for my own childhood cruelties—
the way I taunted Nick Sereno
(*serene*, a thing that neighbor never was,

Dark hungry victim, bird-boned butt of my deceptions . . .
the time I decoyed him out onto the raft
and cut him loose, and jumped.

I cut the frail hemp tether, and off he drifted, quacking fear).
And I forgive the fact that cruelty can circle:
grown, he paid me back one night in a steaming gin mill.

O, this balm of sun!
As if a lifetime's bruises might be balmed!
O, that summer would at last outlast the things to come!

Out on the flooding shellfish beds the Scoters pinwheel,
as if in fun and not in search of food.
I can even forgive the fighter pilots flying

Low as Harriers across the headland.
They flush the drifting Blacks in fear toward me.
In the hot breeze, I can count their single feathers,

Black and blue as birth,
with a seeming whiteness underneath.
Again my sweet-souled dogs look up, perplexed.

They champ their still undulled white puppy teeth.
There is more to all of this than I allow.
Here, in this paradox of weather—

Here for now I let things go,
the mind as light as light upon the wind,
as if here changed and changed into an answer.

Telescope

Light projected lifetimes ago
from farthest stars is arriving now
here where my poor house moans
on its chilling sills and stones
and where I stand, quiet and sleepless,
with only my half-blind dog for witness,
everyone else in slumber.
Silent before such wonders,
I know alone, and inexactly,
the inexact science of memory.
A man who studies things to come
for livelihood tells me in time
there will be a lens which, pointed back
at earth, may show us all the past,
even to our creation.
How little would be the elevation
it needed to show me the people
and places I might have considered crucial:
my young friend Michael drunkenly
hulking over his purple Harley
that swore against the blossoms of May
pinkly dropping around us there
like what we might have taken for flares

of warning, if he had been less proud
and I more equal to warning. I stood
dumb as a dog. You could call it collusion,
or guilt by reason of inaction.
(His head-on into that rushing car
is just now reaching a nearby star.)
With the glass I could also see the feathers
flare on a partridge held by my father,
and the pointer who cocks his head and chatters,
and wants to hunt, and what is the matter?
Around us the last of afternoon falls
on the last stalks standing in autumn fields
as now, by word and look he petitions
me for the slightest recognition.
But I won't hear the argument,
I have no interest in what is meant.
His words are rising into balloons
of white, like those o's you see in cartoons
above a speaker's head.
Turn the lens a hair and he's dead.
There, a guttered candle that flickers
—I simply don't know how to give her
what she begs—in the eye of a girl.
There, my runt chum Ed in a whirl
of agony as I refrain
from choosing him up for some childhood team.
The whirling earth, a galaxy
of scene and soul and silence and need.
A word or two, not much
beyond what I said . . . or a touch—
how little it would have taken
by way of speech or look or action
to change the times I now imagine
in which a silent man or woman,

myself included, would come off better.
But all those moments are fixed forever,
and such a lens no more effective
than memory, no more corrective.

Fall

Carpenter, Mechanic, and I:
it is our yearly hunting trip
to this game-rich, splendid, dirt-poor margin
of Maine. There is always rain and a gale,
and one or two
bluebird days just to break the heart.
We're good at this thing we do,
but for each bird that falls,
three get by us and go
wherever the things that get by us go.

To the realm of baby shoe and milk tooth;
kingdom of traduced early vow,
of the hedge's ghost, humming with rabbit and rodent,
under the mall's macadam. All that seemed
fixed in the eye. I,
according to Mechanic,
is too melancholic. Yes, says Carpenter,
and talks when he ought to be doing.
We all watch the canny Setter, with her nose
like a Geiger counter.

"There's not much gets by *her*,"
we repeat each year, admiring, after she's flashed on point
and *shaaa!*—in redundant wind another grouse flies wild.
Air and ridge and water now all take

the color of week-old blood. Or years-old ink.
We are such friends it's sad.
Not long before we stalk before winter the heavy-horned
bucks that slide past,
spirit-quiet, in spare brush.
Then Carpenter and Mechanic in their loud mackinaws will seem

interruptions on the skyline of the sky's
clean slate. And so will I.

PHILIP LEVINE

Look

The low-built houses of the poor
were all around him, and it
was dawn now, and he was more
awake than not. So it is
a young man begins his life.
Someone, probably his brother,
has quietly closed the front
door, and he feels a sudden gust
of cold air and opens his eyes.
Through the uncurtained window
the great factory sulks in gray
light, there where his mother
must be finishing the night,
her arms crossed and immersed
in the deep, milky wash-basin,
those long and slender arms
that seemed to him as hard
and drawn as a man's, and
now she would be smiling
with one eye closed and blurred
by the first cigarette in hours.
He sits up and lights his first
too and draws the smoke in
as deeply as he can and feels
his long nakedness stretched
out before him, filling the bed
now grown too small for him.
They will pass, mother and son,
on the street, and he will hold

her straight, taut body for
a moment and smell the grease
in her hair and touch her lips
with his, and today he will not
wonder why the tears start and
stall in her eyes and in his.
Today for the first time in
his life he will let his hands
stray across her padded back
and shoulders, feeling them
give and then hold, and he will
not say one word, not *mother*
or *Ruth* or *Goodbye*. If you
are awake in the poor light
of this November, have a look
down at the street that leads
the way you too will have soon
to take. Do you see them there
stopped in each others' arms,
these two who love each other?
Go ahead and look! You wanted
to live as much as they did,
you asked the day to start,
and the day started, but not
because you asked. Forward
or back, they've got no place
to go. No one's blaming you.

Sweet Will

The man who stood beside me
34 years ago this night fell
on to the concrete, oily floor
of Detroit Transmission, and we
stepped carefully over him until
he wakened and went back to his press.

It was Friday night, and the others
told me that every Friday he drank
more than he could hold and fell
and he wasn't any dumber for it
so just let him get up at his
own sweet will or he'll hit you.

"At his own sweet will," was just
what the old black man said to me,
and he smiled the smile of one
who is still surprised that dawn
graying the cracked and broken windows
could start us all to singing in the cold.

Stash rose and wiped the back of his head
with a crumpled handkerchief and looked
at his own blood as though it were
dirt and puzzled as to how
it got there and then wiped the ends
of his fingers carefully one at a time

the way the mother wipes the fingers
of a sleeping child, and climbed back
on his wooden soda-pop case to
his punch press and hollered at all
of us over the oceanic roar of work,
addressing us by our names and nations—

"Nigger, Kike, Hunky, River Rat,"
but he gave it a tune, an old tune,
like "America the Beautiful." And he danced
a little two-step and smiled showing
the four stained teeth left in the front
and took another suck of cherry brandy.

In truth it was no longer Friday,
for night had turned to day as it
often does for those who are patient,
so it was Saturday in the year of '48
in the very heart of the city of man
where your Cadillac cars get manufactured.

In truth all those people are dead,
they have gone up to heaven singing
"Time on My Hands" or "Begin the Beguine,"
and the Cadillacs have all gone back
to earth, and nothing that we made
that night is worth more than me.

And in truth I'm not worth a thing
what with my feet and my two bad eyes
and my one long nose and my breath
of old lies and my sad tales of men
who let the earth break them back,
each one, to dirty blood or bloody dirt.

"Not worth a thing" Just like it was said
at my magic birth when the stars
collided and fire fell from great space
into great space, and people rose one
by one from cold beds to tend a world
that runs on and on at its own sweet will.

At Bessemer

19 years old and going nowhere,
I got a ride to Bessemer and walked
the night road toward Birmingham
passing dark groups of men cursing
the end of a week like every week.
Out of town I found a small grove
of trees, high narrow pines, and I
sat back against the trunk of one
as the first rains began slowly.
South, the lights of Bessemer glowed
as though a new sun rose there,
but it was midnight and another shift
tooled the rolling mills. I must
have slept a while, for someone
else was there beside me. I could
see a cigarette's soft light,
and once a hand grazed mine, man
or woman's I never knew. Slowly
I could feel the darkness fill
my eyes and the dream that came was
of a bright world where sunlight
fell on the long even rows of houses
and I looked down from great height
at a burned world I believed
I never had to enter. When
the true sun rose I was stiff
and wet, and there beside me was
the small white proof that someone
rolled and smoked and left me there
unharmed, truly untouched.
A hundred yards off I could hear
cars on the highway. A life
was calling to be lived, but how
and why I had still to learn.

Jewish Graveyards, Italy

Within a low wall falling away
into dust, a few acres of stones,
wildflowers, tall grasses, weeds.
By the house, firewood stacked
neatly for the winter ahead. Now
it is summer, and even before noon
the heat is rising to stun us all,
the crickets, salamanders, ants.
The large, swart flies circle slowly
in air around something I can't see
and won't be waved away. The old man
who answered the bell and let me in
has gone back to his rocking chair
and sits bareheaded softly whistling
a song I've forgotten. Dove moans,
or something like them, from under
the low, scorched pines, and farther
off the laughter of other birds,
and beyond the birds, the hum
of a distant world still there.
A truck gearing down to enter town,
an auto horn, perhaps the voices
of children leaving school, for it's
almost that time. A low wind
raises the hankie I've knotted
at the corners, and with one hand
I hold it and bend to the names
and say them as slowly as I can.
Full, majestic, vanished names
that fill my mouth and go out
into the densely yellowed air
of this great valley and dissolve

as even the sea dissolves beating
on a stone shore or as love does
when the beloved turns to stone
or dust or water. The old man
rocks and whistles by turns
into the long afternoon, and I
bow again to what I don't know.

SHADE

wild roses bursting
in the branches of low hemlocks, thistles
to which the bees swarm.
I've come out of the heat of the city to rest
in the shade of death,
but at noon there's no more shade in this place
than on the streets.
As for death, I saw only a huge symbolic spider
that refused to scuttle
into a bin of firewood when I snapped my hankie.
The wood was green olive,
the twisting branches stacked in two-foot lengths.
Once upon a time
when even the weather proved too much, I would
close my eyes and find
another weather. The raw azures and corals
of the soul raged across
the great, black pastures of my childhood
at their pleasure.
That was prayer. But now when I open them
I don't find the grave
of the unknown English poet the world scorned
or his friend who lived,
I don't hear the music of a farther life beyond
this life. I hear traffic

not far off. I see small wild daisies climbing
the weeds that sprout
from the grave of Sofia Finzi Hersch, who died
in New Jersey and rests
among her Italian relatives. I feel my legs
cramp in this odd posture,
for I'm kneeling. I feel the cold damp of soil
given back to the earth
before the earth could take it back, and the heat
familiar on my back
bowed in the poor shade of a rusting alder.

RAIN

At the end of a street of rain
there's always a place to find,
a gray rope to pull, a dull ringing
from within, an old frowning woman
shuffling in felt house slippers
to unlock the gate and say nothing.
A rusted barrow in an alcove,
shovels crossed on mounded dirt,
then the sad acres of polished stones
fallen this way and that. I can
stand under an umbrella, a man
in a romance I never finished
come to tell the rain a secret
the living don't want and the dead know:
how life goes on, how seasons pass,
the children grow, and the earth gives
back what it took. My shoes darken.
I move from one cluster of stones
to another studying the names
and dates that tell me nothing I
didn't guess. In sunlight, in moonlight,
or in rain, it's always the same,

whatever truth falls from the sky
as slowly as dust settling in
morning light or cold mist rising
from a river, takes the shape
I give it, and I can't give it any.
A wind will come up if I stand
here long enough and blow the clouds
into smoking shapes of water
and earth. Before the last darkness
rises from the wet wild grasses,
new soft rays of late sunlight
will fall through, promising nothing.
They overflow the luminous thorns
of the roses, they catch fire
for a moment on the young leaves.

Salts and Oils

In Havana in 1948 I ate fried dog
believing it was Peking duck. Later,
in Tampa I bunked with an insane sailor
who kept a .38 Smith and Wesson in his shorts.
In the same room were twins, oilers
from Toledo, who argued for hours
each night whose turn it was
to get breakfast and should he turn
the eggs or not. On the way north
I lived for three days on warm water
in a DC-6 with a burned out radio
on the runway at Athens, Georgia. We sang
a song, "Georgia's Big Behind," and prayed
for WW III and complete, unconditional surrender.
Napping in an open field near Newport News,

I chewed on grass while the shadows of September
lengthened; in the distance a man hammered
on the roof of a hanger and groaned how he
was out of luck and vittles. Bummed a ride
in from Mitchell Field and had beet borsch
and white bread at 34th and 8th Avenue.
I threw up in the alley behind the YMCA
and slept until they turned me out.
I walked the bridge to Brooklyn
while the East River browned below.
A mile from Ebbetts Field, from all
that history, I found Murray, my papa's
buddy, in his greasy truck shop, polishing
replacement parts. Short, unshaven, puffed,
he strutted the filthy aisles,
a tiny Ghengis Khan. He sent out for soup
and sandwiches. The world turned on barley,
pickled meats, yellow mustard, kasha,
rye breads. It rained in October, rained
so hard I couldn't walk and smoke, so I
chewed pepsin chewing gum. The rain
spoiled Armistice Day in Lancaster, Pa.
The open cars overflowed, girls cried,
the tubas and trombones went dumb,
the floral displays shredded, the gutters
clogged with petals. Afterwards had ham
on buttered whole wheat bread, ham
and butter for the first time
on the same day in Zanesville with snow
forecast, snow, high winds, closed roads,
solid darkness before 5 p.m. These were not
the labors of Hercules, these were not
of meat or moment to anyone but me
or destined for story or to learn from
or to make me fit to take the hand

of a toad or a toad princess or to stand
in line for food stamps. One quiet morning
at the end of my thirteenth year a little bird
with a dark head and tattered tail feathers
had come to the bedroom window and commanded
me to pass through the winding miles
of narrow dark corridors and passageways
of my growing body the filth and glory
of the palatable world. Since then I've
been going out and coming back
the way a swallow does with unerring grace
and foreknowledge because all of this
was prophesied in the final, unread book
of the Misrath and because I have to
grow up and because it pleases me.

PAUL MARIANI

Matadero, Riley & Company

A perfectly useless concentration:
the way one poet put it, describing
the state of the art. And what good,
this Good Friday, to stir up cold ash
to find this single image glowing:
the one circling the other like a jackal,
hackles bristling, his left fist feinting
first then slamming to his heart's content.

For the past two days troubled by Riley's
shifting image, faster than the bull-
necked Matadero, jabbing again and yet
again at the bloody head, playing it
like a cat clawing at a shredded ball.
I still see myself watching
from the safety of my front lawn, eyes fixed
across the street, my left hand gripping

the cold handlebars of my battered
Schwinn, the wobbly kickstand trying
to support it, my right arm cradling
the bag of groceries for my mother.
I stare at the solid ring of boys
watching Riley and Matadero,
expanding and contracting like
a pumping heart to let Matadero

stumble as he needs. Only
the crack of Riley's fists against
the other's face breaks the silence.

I would make more sense of all
of this, but the names are gone,
even from the small black-and-white
Kodak shots I have of them,
though one (which face I cannot now

remember) is a cop out on the Island
and another sells sneakers down
in Tampa, and one's a coach and one
did time my brother tells me for breaking
someone's neck in a barroom down in Merrick,
and two at least are dead. Most
of them are married now (and some of them
divorced) with teenage children of

their own: working class stiffs
who bought the dream without the substance—
myself among them if they would count
me in—the wops, the poles, the micks
giving way with time up and down
the sycamore and maple-tented streets
to even newer families with names
like Rodriguez, Alicea, and Rivera.

A shadow world only, and yet
the scars still itch. The eyes close
again in tired meditation and again
they flinch before that grin of Matadero's,
who waited for me as I clambered up
the far steps of the piss-soaked
tunnel running under the Long
Island railroad tracks, that graffiti-

riddled rite of adolescent passage.
How often I used to pray for him
to die. At least to be delivered

from his grip. And then, with the clear-
eyed logic of some Jacobean tragedy,
here was Riley catching up at last
with Matadero and jabbing at
his face, again, again. And this

was no clean, first-strike John
Wayne kill, the kind I once saw
a cheetah make in *Life*, when his teeth
and jaws crunched the cornered baboon's
skull. No, this was cat-and-mouse,
a jab, a jab and then another,
while the arms of Matadero hung,
too bone-weary useless to keep even

the blows from landing on his bleeding
eyes, his broken nose, disfigured
lips. On that cold March morning
back there thirty years ago,
while the random clouds drifted
piecemeal overhead, the age of Riley
replaced the short-lived age of Matadero.
And yet, what pleasure in revenge?

For months after Riley and company
pursued the beaten loser, left now
without a friend. Even I walked about
in Riley's shadow with impunity.
But in the white waste of time it all
sinks down again to *ecce homo*,
behold one more human being beaten,
this one on the playing fields of Mineola.

Sarcophagus

Anger so hot, so thick & clotted,
it drowned out even expletives & grunts.
They wouldn't and they wouldn't
oh God they wouldn't

until the tide of blood had risen
to my eyes & I had damned them,
punishing the poor coughing Pinto
all the way to Greenfield to get the lime

myself & saw the two of them
as I shot back into the driveway (denting
the goddamn crankcase as I did it)
cutting the lawn at last: that undulating

seagreen half an acre they said they couldn't
&, no, they wouldn't ever do. *Get out*,
I shouted, *get the hell out now*, as in Massaccio's
expulsion from the garden glimpsed behind

the metal scaffold railing there in the chapel
at Firenze, so that they dropped the rake
& left the mower there mid-swath as I began to lug
the bags of lime myself that squatted

in the trunk like lopped shark's carcasses
& caught the bag against the indifferent
metal latch, lime exploding over hair
& nose & tongue & unsuspecting eyes,

this cool, sweet, flesh-eating lime,
& put my head against the raised
trunk lid, a clown in white face, at last
defeated by my anger, so that both my sons could see

their father's nakedness as they tread water
out of there, too scared to help, too smart
at least to laugh. Then something deep within
my battered dogbrain whimpered to let go & die,

until a great sargasso frigid briny calm
washed over me & I was slipping
through the makeshift ice hole
into the stunned silence of a bluegreen grey

of ribbed & mottled shapes. No gawky flatfoot
wobblers now, the massive emperor penguins
sleek as ninepins hurtled past me in balletic
arabesque above my head as they skimmed

the underbelly of the floe, indifferent
to my presence. I must have turned, then,
scissoring down into the purple depths
sequestered there to witness squid and horny mollusk,

translucent foetal shrimp, the blue
& phosphorescent spiderforms & worms that palpitate
at zero centigrade plus two: here
at the very edge of life itself

where Dante thought the Mount
of Purgatory rose, the anti-mask
of hell's imploding core, the purple-blackened
bands that signify the depths and then the void.

Far above I caught the airhole icing over,
saw the watching shadow figures who had been
my sons wait until the hole filled in
then turn to other voices calling from the shore.

Alone at last, I stared into those depths
along the spectral edge of twilight and caught

the figure of my father standing at the county
airport gate alone this April, hands folded,

as if rooted, while the twin-engined Beechcraft
labored up & up the unfamiliar purple wetlands
of the Eastern Shore against the coming night
& I waved belated recognition though I knew

he could not see me. *Forgive me father*,
I heard something in me breaking, as now
the lime began to burn the sockets of my eyes.
Forgive me for the grief I know I caused you.

But the depths had grown beyond my telling,
where a face had waited all these many years
drifting in the frigid stillness. It was limewhite
& seemed at home here in the perfect zero cold.

News That Stays News

I don't know but it might have been
the summer of '58, July, time thickening
or thinning the way heavy fog will on a slick
country road, the headlights spattering
as if they'd hit a wall. What I do remember
though as if it were yesterday is my father

down in the filter room under the pool
at Baumann's Summer Day Camp trying to fix
the leaking chlorine tank and fiddling
with the valves and meters, me standing
on the metal grid ladder over him my hand
on the drum door and then the thick yellow gas

seeping up to catch him staggering sideways
like some Bowery drunk gagging for air as he made it
up the steps his green mouth retching so that
he was straight out for two days. All I caught
was a mouthful of the stuff and that left me
weak-kneed and my lungs rasping, enough of a taste

so that it still smells every time I dive
into a motel pool. It was mustard gas killed
my mother's father and don't let anyone tell me
different, though it took fifteen years to do the job,
the cloud hugging the shelled ground as it rolled
in over that no-man's land with the dawn breeze

before it hunkered down on those trapped there
in the trench without their masks. Gas. Gas.
Outlawed in the twenties and then so many times again.
And now, after the Army has at last admitted
to the effects of Agent Orange on our own boys
(to say nothing of what we did to tree and Cong),

the other side is seeding its own rain of terror,
yellow spoilt-grain toxins rocketlaunched by Jeep
and helicopter into Laos and Kampuchea, Yemen
and Afghanistan, dumbstruck villagers including
pigs and babies, left to drown in their own blood,
faces gone black from that internal strangulation,

so that I sit on the edge of my easychair before
the T.V. screen and pound the arm rest
with my clenched right fist, again, again, until
my sons start up, one from his comic book the other
from his world history homework, each wondering
what all this new commotion is about.

North/South

For Bob Pack

In the long run for both of us
it will be the willow darkening
in a northern twilight
as the dominant key of winter

reasserts itself. As even now
in late August outside this window
the small birds hesitate among
the branches before they arc

their bodies south for the three
days' flight above the darkening
waters. Angel-winged they turn,
before they lock on their own

essential homings. Or, to see it
from your perspective: flight
to a southernmost extreme. Robert,
for whom if not for you

could I feel this bond, your north
anchoring my still-vexed south?
Even these so-called free-verse
lines arc in a double *pas-de-deux*

pan-foot, goat-foot rocking back
and forth, playing counter
to that granite bass of yours.
You grin that flinty grin glistening

in the wintry air you call
your home now, made native
by the will itself. "You still
dance a little crazy," you say,

"but no cop could say you didn't
toe the line. What *you* have
is a case of free form hurtling
after form. Count yourself among

the blessèd ones who still have
something to go home to." Robert,
who was it warned us both to work
while there was still light enough

to work with, knowing the long night
must needs be coming on? The night:
when all hands must willy-nilly rest,
the last line edging into granite

or the upturn of the wind, the same wind
which turns the feathers of the small birds
up as they chatter in the branches.
They too must sense the great change

coming on and so begin again while there is
still time to test their wings, half shaped
by years of trial and half again by luck, before
they turn at last into the very air itself.

Goodnight Irene

I am ten and a half and my father
has let me come to work with him again
at Scotty's Esso in Mineola, the wood
and plaster tudor building three blocks
east of the pseudo-bauhaus boy's
Catholic highschool, from which one day
I will venture out to try the priesthood on
(and fail) knowing it is not
for me when I start keeping (against
Brother Clyde's injunction) a marker
in my physics textbook beside the picture
of the lovely in the armlength cashmere sweater
with those swelling upturned breasts.
And from beneath the row of fanbelts
hanging spiderlike I can see the neon
Rheingold sign pulse dully in the doorway
of the Colonial Bar & Grill
where thirteen years from now Wilbur
will split my upper lip with an ice cube
flung across the smoky underwater room
before my brother Walter can hit him
easy with that cross-body block of his
while I reel off my drunky speech to these
my friends a week before my marriage.
But for now I am inside the station
listening to my father singing chorus
after chorus of "Irene, goodnight, Irene,
I'll see you in my dreams," seeing only
part of his face down in the grease pit,
the wrench in his clenched right fist,
his hooded lamp throwing fitful shadows
all across the wall, as he performs
whatever mysteries it is he does to cars.

Useless even to my father, I watch
the yellow sunlight blocked in squares
drift east across the blackened bench
where two halfmoon brakedrums cup
the ballpeen hammer as in a Juan Gris
still-life, the calendar (gift of *Kelly's*
Tires) still turned to August, above which
the cellophane with the nightie
painted on it conceals the underlying
mystery of the lady kneeling there
who smiles frankly at me.
And now the warm smell of leaking
kerosene from the thumbsmeared
darkgreen fifty-gallon tin as I wipe
the opaque bluegreen bottles
of reconstituted oil for the old
"baraccas" as my father calls them.
On the box radio above the wheezy Coke machine
word drones Marines are fighting in a place
called Seoul but there is trouble even
closer home and soon someone is singing
once again the song my father
also loves to sing, "Irene, Goodnight."
And I think of mother back in Levittown
teaching Walter how to read
as my sisters go on playing dolly,
the younger one putting her wedding dress
on backwards while I help my father
put all the bolts into one coffee can
and all the nuts into the other.
And now my Uncle Vic (the one
the strokes choked off three years ago)
grabs his grease-clogged rag
and mutters as he strides out
into the sun to gas up some revved-up Ford,

the static gargling high above the engine's
macho rumble while my father goes on working
on the underbelly of the car
where the light is coming from,
singing still again "Goodnight, Irene."
But my mother's name is not Irene
her name is Harriet and I wonder why
my father wants to see this other lady
in his dreams but I cannot ask
and will not even know what it is
I want to ask until I am older
than he is this September afternoon in 1950
and now the tears well up for him
and for my mother and myself as I turn
to look back down into the empty pit
to tell him now I understand.

WILLIAM MATTHEWS

The Accompanist

Don't play too much, don't play
too loud, don't play the melody.
You have to anticipate her
and to subdue yourself.
She used to give me her smoky
eye when I got boisterous,
and I learned to play on tip-
toe and to play the better half
of what I might. I don't like
to complain, though I notice
that I get around to it somehow.
We made good music and a living,
both, and I loved to hear her
sing, practice or on stage
or even from her tub. She'd sing
like a fast train on thin ice
and deliver all that cargo cross
the lake. I also loved the times
we found the same right music.
Some people like to say with a wink
in their voices how playing
like that is partly sexual.
Well, I could tell you a tale
or two, and I've heard the records
Lester cut with Billie Holiday
and all that rap, and it's
partly sexual but it's mostly
practice and music. As for

partly sexual, I'll take wholly
sexual anyday, but that's a duet
and we're talking accompaniment.
It's like in *Reckless blues*: Bessie
Smith sings out "Daddy," and Louis
Armstrong plays back "Daddy" as clear
through his horn as if he'd spoken it.
But it's her daddy and her story,
don't you know? When you play it
you become your part in it, one
of her beautiful troubles, and then,
however much music can do this,
part of her consolation. And well,
that's always part of what you are,
don't you know, but the bulk of you
is like the music you live by,
a kind of unrecorded history.

Prolific

The boy Mozart could compose,
he bragged in a letter to Leopold,
as copiously "as sows piss"
and freely as a boy's ink flows.

When you're his age, art's
what's left over from experience.
Later, desire is what the heart
can neither hold nor spend,

and then art seems a distil-
lation; isn't this clouded water
a history of appetite writ small,
of consequence, of laughter?

As much as you can strew
makes up the body of your work.
By wasting away, like a moon,
you grow thin, but what you were

is something else by now: sky,
days beyond recall, beautiful
music composed by the lonely
but performed ensemble.

Lucky and Unlucky

mean the same thing, like flammable and inflammable.
Four crows gabble on the peak of my roof; then three
flop languidly aloft—it's 45° this morning, but they
move with the malarial torpor of the poorest tropics—

like black papers rising from a fire. The mountain ash
at the edge of the park is where they'll pass most of the day,
arguing Friday night's high school football games, maybe,
or economics, or anything that brims and seethes over

its edges, like our ability to describe our lives,
or the almost vascular urgency to do it. The one who holds
back, what about it? When they were a quartet, they all
made a music incomplete in its parts, and now this one

blue-black-ink-shiny sentinel, each of its eyes as big as some
hummingbirds, squats like a charred pear with a beak
on the nest of its own silence, which is also incomplete,
or, depending on how you think of it, complete.

Clearwater Beach, Florida

Each dockpost comes with a pelican
who seems to my eight-year-old eye
to be a very distinguished bat. And then
one languidly unrumples itself and flies
off like a purposeful overcoat.

Signs on the causeway warn not to eat
the oleander leaves. A new place means
new poisons. And the palmetto grass,
and the topknotted bromeliads, and
the jellyfish like clouds of clear brains

trailing rain. . . . The scenery is in another
language and I'm still besotted by
my own, half books and half Ohio.
A children's work is never done, so
I'm up early, stubbing my whole foot

on the sprinkler caps in the rosetted
grass. Is it too early to cry? Do I talk
too much? What does it mean to be full
of yourself, or on vacation?
There's something from church—a living

coal on the tongue—I remember. What's
a dead coal? It won't be breakfast
until the grown-ups break the blur and crust
of sleep and come downstairs, and al-
ready, once again, I'm given to language.

Though how could they have saved me?
I'm staunch in the light-blanched yard

and they're in sleep, through which their last
dreams of the morning percolate,
and I'm in the small fort of my sunburnt body.

Photo of the Author with a Favorite Pig

Behind its snout like a huge button,
like an almost clean plate, the pig

looks candid compared to the author,
and why not? He has a way with words,

but the unspeakable pig, squat
and foursquare as a bathtub,

squints frankly. Nobody knows
the trouble it's seen, this rained-out

pig roast, this ham escaped into
its corpulent jokes, its body of work.

The author is skinny and looks serious,
as if wondering what to say to the pig,

which is fat and looks funny,
as if it knows, but can't say.

JAMES MERRILL

The Parnassians

Theirs was a language within ours, a loge
Hidden by bee-stitched hanging from the herd.
The mere exchanged glance between word and word
Took easily the place, the privilege,
Of words themselves. Here therefore all was tact.
Pairs at first blush ill-matched, like *turd* or *monstrance*,
Tracing their cousinage by consonants,
Communed, ecstatic, through the long entr'acte.

Without our common meanings, though, that world
Would have slid headlong to apocalypse.
We'd built the Opera, changed the scenery, trod
Grapes for the bubbling flutes mild fingers twirled;
As footmen, by no eyelid's twitch betrayed
Our scorn and sound investment of their tips.

JUDITH MOFFETT

The Price of Wildness

The wild child rolling naked in the snow
With wordless joy, the tame child with his sled
And snowsuit shouting "Dad, hey, watch me Dad!"—
Each, in his own way blessed, can never know

The other's luck. Words are the price of wildness
That pure, and wildness the fair price of words.
Lord Greystoke speaking in the House of Lords,
Parrying qualms and barbs with courteous mildness,

OR Tarzan sleeping bare-ass in a crotch,
Fat haunch of something bloody in his clutch:

Choose one. Mowgli could not be Mowgli, ever;
The mythic twins could not have founded Rome.
A door seals in the self: nobody home.
Language, like love, comes early or comes never.

Hear Now the Fable of the Missing Link:

Sunrise. The weedy rubblefield turns pink.
Out of an archway several creatures bound,
long shadows gliding on the fractured ground
like ghosts. As daylight strengthens, we can see
two seem great dogs and one's a chimpanzee
and one's a naked boy with tangled hair.
None makes a sound, but you could almost swear

that they're in touch, watching how dogs and ape
look, often, to the boy. This rubblescape
is crawling rats and roaches, meaning each
has snacked on something by the time all reach
the river. Now abruptly there's a change.
The child stops, stiffens, in his eyes a strange
expression lights. His comrades realize
what's up at once, and halt; three pairs of eyes
fix on the boy and never leave his face
till he goes scrambling down the bluff, a place
of tumbled steel and concrete lashed with vines.
Is that a voice? One of the dog-things whines
then howls, the ape starts hooting; there's a man!
He sees the chimp, who looks Gargantuan,
and screams, and then he spots the child. "Thank God!
I'm trapped here, broke my leg I think. The squad
missed me last night, I guess nobody heard—"
He stops. The boy still hasn't said a word.
"Oh, Christ, you're not a *loonie*, kid? Oh fuck,
I might have known. Of all the rotten luck!
That's it, then." No it's not; the child moves near
and crouches, smiling. Through his pain and fear
the man takes in that though the boy's bare knees
are padded with immense callosities
the hands that stroke his pale jaw and the palm
laid on his brow feel soft, the eyes are calm,
intelligent—a star bursts in the mind
of the astonished victim, who's struck blind
at once with tears. The boy stands up and puts
his arms around the chimp, whose nervous hoots
stop instantly; after a moment they
start heaving chunks of rubbleslide away.
The dogs are digging too, and soon they've got
the man—whose leg is badly bruised but not
broken, luckily, after all—dug loose.

He's dazed, of course. Again the boy bends close,
again the starburst—"I can hear you *think*!
I thought you said—you'll help me down to drink,
bring food, the ape won't hurt me—is that true?
You understand my thoughts? And yours come through?
My God"—he's crying now—"*you understand
exactly how I feel.*" The boy's dark hand
grips his, then helps him rise; a grin, a nod,
they're crippling toward the water. "Oh my God . . ."
The chimp goes knuckling down beside the boy,
the wolves lie down in customary joy.

FREDERICK MORGAN

The Christmas Tree

In the quiet house, on a morning of snow,
the child stares at the Christmas Tree.
He wonders what there is to know

behind the tinsel and the glow—
behind what he's been taught to see
in the quiet house, on mornings of snow,

when he's snug indoors with nowhere to go
and mother and father have let him be:
he wonders if there's more to know

about their bright, triumphant show
than he's been told. Is the brave Tree,
so proud in the house on this morning of snow,

all that it seems? He gathers no
assurance from its silent glee
and fears there must be more to know

than one poor child can learn. If so,
what stake may he claim in the mystery?
He stares from the house at the falling snow
and wonders how he'll ever know.

1904

The things they did together, no one knew.
It was late June. Behind the old wood-shed
wild iris was in blossom, white and blue,
but what those proud ones did there no one knew,
though some suspected there were one or two
who led the others where they would be led.
Years passed—but what they did there no one knew,
those summer children long since safely dead.

Song

In Ireland, in Ireland
where ancient deaths are green
they sing in choir the ancient airs
of gods and kings and queens
and ride in curraghs on blue bays
whose waters sparkle all the day
in gem-stones a fierce queen might wear
along her arms or in her hair
in Ireland, in Ireland
where death is always green

In Ireland, in Ireland
where ancient deaths are green
they dance and drink all day
in a heedless kind of way
as though life held no perils
or pains that they need fear,
as though death never would be coming—
and when night falls at last

they take their dark delight
in the young limber girls
the fine prancing women,
all night they dance and have delight
in one another's appetites
until the sun, returning
renews his ancient light
on Ireland, on Ireland,
where I have never been

HOWARD MOSS

Heaven

There are so many ideas of heaven
All of them but one must be wrong,
And even that one tainted, I suspect,
By the fanaticism of place and time,
A desert culture producing a fertile
Valley and a valley a mountaintop.

The angels walk on sponge in summer dreams
In a casual deportment of wings and heels,
Clad in Bedouin cloth or long, striped skirts,
Like a waltzer of a century ago
Leaning across a Victorian sofa
To say, "Dancing—how it stirs the air!"

An Italian looking closely at a shoe
Discovered nails could be disguised as wood—
Parquet derived from that, the waltz as well,
Each providing a means of gliding,
And the chandelier—did it invent its highlights,
Or crystal flame and blue the chandelier
Sailing above the whirling dancers?

Does heaven pay back its brave disclaimers
With a hard retribution at the end,
The devil saying, "So you didn't believe
In me—well, take a look at this!"?
The swooning damosel, the sickened swain
Suddenly finding eternity is real,

Even if it is nothingness, a cloud of time,
Or a long vacation hardly remembered
Whose returning sojourner comes back to say,
"It rained, it rained all the time I was there."

It

It was a question of whether it couldn't
See you or you see it, that surface
That was more than a surface, crooning its jokes,
Like "Hello, stranger!" and "Sir, you're up!"

And sometimes, "Darling, where have you been?"
Cosying back to you in your bathrobe,
Slightly sick and wanting you home
To give it hot tea and toast in bed,

Wanting you there, and I mean always,
Waiting for hours until you'd appear
To give it life, some reason for
Existing at all, it would often say,

Watching you shave into a snowy
Newness of flesh, watching you comb
Hair there was less and less of, swearing
"I'll never breathe a word of this to anyone,"

Confessing its hopes only to you:
"Clean me, please. Or dirty me further.
Or break me in two. Or make me whole.
I'll never leave you. Never, never."

CAROL MUSKE

Immunity

Issa's little daughter, Sato-jo,
on all fours in this haiku, laughs!
She is seven months, by Western count,
my daughter's age, when he makes her immortal.

Annie splashes in her red tub
on the grass and I read further:
a second haiku for Sato-jo,
dead of smallpox before the year is done.

He stood over her as she began to fail.
Near dawn, light surrounded him
like a moat. The kind of light
I used to believe came from God,

at the hour when light does nothing
desultory: falling expressly on
the woman shaking out her long black hair
or on the healthy child waking up.

I remember it shining in my mother's
bedroom, through a Japanese screen
thin as a pressed flower. She loved
that artist who hated disorder—

his raging hurricane a study in restraint,
the sea rising in white scrolls,
the fleeing figures composed in their terror.
Issa touched her hair, he closed her eyes.

It was long ago. There was no such thing
as immunity. Not the mind's temporary
rescue of itself nor the needle pressing
its small safe deaths into circulation.

What he felt
is in the silence between these haiku;
two clearly opposed notions of perfection.
The baby opens in his hand like a fan,

laughing, so exact that nothing prepares us
for the second poem, which follows, observing
how autumn winds scatter the red flowers
she loved to pluck. It too is precise, each

blossom lost, accounted for. He says nothing
of the first possessiveness of this age.
How they praise each thing, then let it go,
conditionally. He says nothing of the kite

bearing the name of the child running
below it or of the line unravelling upward
to the hook in the sky that snags and holds
immune to anything we do on earth.

It was long ago. Syllable by syllable,
I go back. I wrap her in a towel.
I carry her in my arms.
Now her death belongs to me.

Which is why she smiles so happily,
why she will live forever.

LEONARD NATHAN

Just Looking, Thank You

And when suddenly it hit me
that I would never get taller
or wiser or learn Greek
or Hebrew for a proper blessing
or prayer, never interpret
birds for humans or humans
for humans, never hear
the Word for Truth, never
get the first prize or be kissed
for courage, never be more
than the third (if that) person
to be contacted in case
of an emergency,
only a guilty bystander
who didn't get the facts straight
and who envied the truly good
and the lucky,
          I was not sad,
merely a little subdued,
feeling the spirit warmly
dissolve in my flesh like soap
in bathwater, and the food
placed before me then,
even the mashed potatoes,
became intensely personal,
and the stars over my head
unimportant except
as somehow necessary
to the local situation,

and the wars abroad something
to measure indifference by,
and you, the same as always—
turned sidewise with your own
occult obsession, and I felt
like a man in a hiding place
from the wind, or like a shadow
of a rock in a weary land,
secure in the dry lull
or depression between cause
and effect, for whom eating
mashed potatoes was OK,
and OK also allowing
the birds to mean nothing,
the humans to mean whatever
they mean, or so I believe
I believe—and just looking,
thank you, just looking.

The Fall

Tom, working thirty storeys up,
scaffolded against a wide window,
sees his faint reflection in the glass
and through it, sees, as through his own ghost,
a board room carpeted in blue and bronze,
a long teak table running down its length
at which eleven men, moving their lips,
confer in silence. This to Tom means nothing.

He's got along without a meaning well
enough till now. He knows his job and knows
never to look below. Just behind

the man whose frown cooly commands the table
from its head, a slender girl is poised
cradling folders in her arms, ready
to serve. She's neatly dressed, no beauty, true,
but finely wrought in her uncalled-for presence.

He doesn't mean it to, but her quick look
comes up and locks on his a long instant
before it falls, and that is all it needs
for both to know, and Tom to feel under him
a sudden nothing, a sudden need to grab
a rope with his free hand. That she is gone
when he looks up again, hardly matters.
A partial vision changes anything.

It's bad enough that towers now needle up
below. Nowhere is safe. The woods outside
the city conceal death, and his own body,
so fragile in itself, inside itself
conceals hostile cells, and those eleven—
what evil are they planning for poor Tom?
And there's this brittle watery ghost. My God,
he pities it. It now means everything.

Carrying On

At the next table, two carry on
over coffee and without love,
as another pair on the bridge whisper,
as a carp or shadow of a carp
idles deep in an umber pool,
at one with itself and without love,

and without love the doctor diagnoses
while the patient bravely hears and without it
the dog barks a warning, the pilot
safely brings down the wounded plane,
the dying hawthorn blossoms again,
and you tell me what has to be told,
and without love the law of gravity
holds, although I feel the ground
fall weakly away without love,
but without it much yet can be done,
and even peace be made, the peace
of knowing without love what needs
to be known, as the carp at one with itself
knows, or those two now going by
seem to know, holding hands
sadly for some reason, while darkness
swirls around their knees and the streetlamps
flare on like the round yellow eyes
of a huge night creature waking
without love to light us someplace
we have for too long avoided,
an empty cup, our very own,
waiting there for us to fill it,
a cat curled in the warm dusk
of a kitchen, dreaming without love,
waiting for us anyway.

JOHN FREDERICK NIMS

Gravity

Mildest of all the powers of earth: no lightnings
For her—maniacal in the clouds. No need for
Signs with their skull and crossbones, chain-link gates:
Danger! Keep Out! High Gravity! she's friendlier.
Won't nurse—unlike the magnetic powers—repugnance;
Would reconcile, draw close: her passion's love.

No terrors lurking in her depths, like those
Bound in the buzzing strongbox of the atom,
Terrors that, loosened, turn the hills vesuvian,
Trace in cremation where the cities were.

No, she's our quiet mother, sensible.
But therefore down-to-earth, not suffering
Fools who play fast and loose among the mountains,
Who fly in her face, or, drunken, clown on cornices.

She taught our ways of walking. Her affection
Adjusted the morning grass, the sands of summer
Until our soles fit snug in each, walk easy.
Holding her hand, we're safe. Should that hand fail,
The atmosphere we breathe would turn hysterical,
Hiss with tornadoes, spinning us from earth
Into the cold unbreathable desolations.

Yet there—in fields of space—is where she shines,
Ring-mistress of the circus of the stars,
Their prancing carousels, their ferris wheels
Lit brilliant in celebration. Thanks to her
All's gala in the galaxy.

                              Down here she
Walks us just right, not like the jokey moon
Burlesquing our human stride to kangaroo hops,
Not like vast planets, whose unbearable mass
Would crush us in a bearhug to their surface
And under the surface, flattened. No: deals fairly.
Makes happy each with each: the willow bend
Just so, the acrobat land true, the keystone
Nestle in place for bridge and for cathedral.
Lets us pick up—or mostly—what we need:
Rake, bucket, stone to build with, logs for warmth,
The fallen fruit, the fallen child . . . ourselves.

Instructs us too in honesty: our jointed
Limbs move awry and crisscross, gawky, thwart;
She's all directness and makes that a grace,
All downright passion for the core of things,
For rectitude, the very ground of being:
Those eyes are levelled where the heart is set.

See, on the tennis court this August day:
How, beyond human error, she's the one
Whose will the bright balls cherish and obey
—As if in love. She's tireless in her courtesies
To even the klutz (knees, elbows all a-tangle),
Allowing his poky serve Euclidean whimsies,
The looniest lob its joy: serene parabolas.

Elegy

For Marion, for Jane

I

DEATH AND THE MAIDEN

Were you, as old prints have shown,
armor over props of bone,
scythe like scorpion tail a-sway,
here's a word or two I'd say:

When you met that lady now
—her of the amused cool brow—
which of you with more an air
carried off the occurrence there?
Held—the buoyant head so high—
every fascinated eye?
Stole, as half in mischief too,
scenes *you* strutted front to do?

Which at last, when curtains met,
had us leaning forward yet
in the dark?—to breathe and rise,
odd elation in our eyes?

II

"ONE DAY ANYONE DIED I GUESS"

Here she lies, poor dancing head,
in the world we know of, dead.
Every sense avers: The End.
Yet we're hedging (who'd pretend
our five portholes on the night
logged the seven oceans quite?)
hedging: past a world in stream,
past the learned journal's dream

(quark or quasar, beta ray),
what's that glimmer? limbs at play?
Something there? a curtain stirred?
Laughter, far and teasing, heard?

Where such awesome laws are set,
Honey, misbehaving yet?

Hospital Breakfast: With Grace After

I

Waking in drifts of whiteness! head to toe
I'm a white sheet, with all but nose below.
Toes ripple, push, make corners; the sheet pulls tight
Until I'm hemmed in a box here, with four right
Angles and four straight edges, as if I lay
Chalky—

A skirt swirls. And the breakfast tray!

All's orange: dawn at the window, juice I drink.
"Carols of Florida in that golden ink,"
Croons fever, looney. And egg-yolks bobble, most
Like the sun's globe through cirrus. Tussle of toast
That tugs in the teeth. Blonde slinky marmalade—

Lord, what a world the Lord of matter made!

Breakfast—that daily "He is risen!"—swirls
Its color, tang, aroma—cozy as girls
Leaning bare shoulders over, warm hair loose . . .

In hen-fruit such epiphany? Joy in juice?

We, trivial, live by trifles. Froth: our race
Vague as a drift of atoms, in blind space?
Earth offers "neither joy, nor love, nor light,
Nor certitude . . ."

Was Arnold *real*?

Not quite.

Let's venture—for what's to lose?—a breakfast prayer
To the great Thought that dreamed us—if it's there.
St. Peter once went surfing and he scored
Riding his big feet only—look, no board!
Once, strong souls walked on water; were ultra-tough
Qualm-free and wobble-proof all-weather stuff.

We're not like those. But, wreathed in gulls and kelp,
Would ruffle the tidal shallows. Peter, help,
Help us to scrabble over wrack and sand
Alongshore toward—

some distant lighthouse?—

and

To dangle (though water-walkers all are gone),
Our toes in the froth and glamors of the dawn.

SHARON OLDS

I See My Girl

When I see you off to camp, I see you
bending your neck to the weight of your cello, I
see your small torso under the
load of your heavy knapsack the way a
boulder would rest on the body of a child, and
suddenly I see your goodness, the weight of your
patient dogged goodness as you slog your
things to the plane, you look like a small-boned
old lady from darkest Europe
going toward steerage, carrying all the family goods.
Suddenly the whole airport is full of your goodness, your
thin hair looks whittled down by goodness, your
pale face looks drained of blood, your
upward look looks like the look of
someone lying under a stone.
For so long I prayed you would be good,
prayed you would not be anything like Hitler as
I as a child feared I was like Hitler—but I
didn't mean this, the oppression of goodness, the
deadness. You ask for something to eat
and my heart leaps up, I take off your backpack and we
lean your cello against a chair and
then I can sit and watch you eat chocolate pudding,
spoonful after careful spoonful, your
tongue moving slowly over the mixture in
deep pleasure, *Oh it's good, Mom,*
it's good, you beam, and the air around your face
shines with the dark divided shining of goodness.

The Month of June: 13½

As my daughter approaches graduation and
puberty at the same time, at her
own calm deliberate serious rate,
she begins to kick up her heels, jazz out her
hands, thrust out her hip-bones, chant
I'm great! I'm great! She feels 8th grade coming
open around her, a chrysalis cracking and
letting her out, it falls behind her and
joins the other husks on the ground,
7th grade, 6th grade, the
purple rind of 5th grade, the
hard jacket of 4th when she had so much pain,
3rd grade, 2nd, the dim cocoon of
1st grade back there somewhere on the path, and
kindergarten like a strip of thumb-suck blanket
taken from the actual blanket they wrapped her in at birth.
The whole school is coming off her shoulders like a
cloak unclasped, and she dances forth in her
jerky sexy child's joke dance of
self, self, her throat tight and a
hard new song coming out of it, while her
two dark eyes shine
above her body like a good mother and a
good father who look down and
love everything their baby does, the way she
lives their love.

Cambridge Elegy

For Henry Averell Gerry, 1941 – 1960

I hardly know how to speak to you now,
you are so young now, closer to my daughter's age
than mine—but I have been there and seen it, and must
tell you, as the seeing and hearing
spell the world into the deaf-mute's hand.
The tiny dormer windows like the ears of a fox, like the
long row of teats on a pig, still
perk up over the Square, though they're tearing up the
street now, as if digging a grave,
the shovels shrieking on stone like your car
sliding along on its roof after the crash.
How I wanted everyone to die if you had to die,
how sealed into my own world I was,
deaf and blind. What can I tell you now,
now that I know so much and you are a
freshman still, drinking a quart of orange juice and
playing three sets of tennis to cure a hangover, such an
ardent student of the grown-ups! I can tell you
we were right, our bodies were right, life was
really going to be that good, that
pleasurable in every cell.
Suddenly I remember the exact look of your body, but
better than the bright corners of your eyes, or the
light of your face, the rich Long Island
puppy-fat of your thighs, or the slick
chino of your pants bright in the corners of my eyes, I
remember your extraordinary act of courage in
loving me, something which no one but the
blind and halt had done before. You were
fearless, you could drive after a sleepless night
just like a grown-up, and not be afraid, you could
fall asleep at the wheel easily and

never know it, each blond hair of your head—and they were
thickly laid—put out like a filament of light,
twenty years ago. The Charles still
slides by with that ease that made me bitter when I
wanted all things hard as your death was hard;
wanted all things broken and rigid as the
bricks in the sidewalk or your love for me
stopped cell by cell in your young body.
Ave—I went ahead and had the children,
the life of ease and faithfulness, the
palm and the breast, every millimeter of delight in the body,
I took the road we stood on at the start together, I
took it all without you as if
in taking it after all I could most
honor you.

CAROLE OLES

Preparing for Weather

Each time I send you into the sky
where money is made
I let you die.
It has little to do with the weather.

I settle the will, stare
into your closet, dispose of suits,
push some matters away until later.
An instant father, I can
advise the children without argument.
I have all the answers,

plus your half
of the queen-size bed, and
the nocturnal silence I elbowed you for
now an acreage too vast
to survey or build on.

Now you are a statue in the public garden
forever posed as *husband*
the way accident cast you.
You are among the perfect dead.
On my lunch hour I sit on the bench,
almost touching your bronze fingers
like Michelangelo near God.

I am just out of black,
beginning to sing in the shower,
when the door opens and someone like you is home

—poised for ribbons and balloons,
asking what happened
while he was gone.

To a Daughter at Fourteen
Forsaking the Violin

All year, Mozart went under
the sea of rock punk reggae
that crashed into your room every
night and wouldn't recede however
I sandbagged our shore
and swore to keep the house dry.
Your first violin, that halfsize
rented model, slipped out of tune
as you played Bach by ear
Suzuki method with forty other virtuosos
who couldn't tie their shoes.
Then such progress: your own
fiddle, the trellised notes you read,
recitals where I sat on hard chairs.
Your playing made me the kid.
If I had those fingers! . . .
Five of yours grasped my pinky,
the world before you grew teeth.
O.K. They're your fingers.
To paint the nails of, put rings on,
hold cigarettes in, make obscene
gestures or farewells with.

Between Talcy and Mer

Here 40 years ago on moonless nights
pilots cut their engines
and Allies parachuted down.
I know from movies
the farmer's lantern, the password.

In July now, irrigation sprays
fan the fields with light,
tiny mirrors that rise, arc, shatter
the heat-stunned afternoon.

Along the unswerving road
someone has planted roses—for miles,
alternate sides the way a flowergirl
scatters petals for the bride and groom.
The French are like this with roads.
Everywhere ranks of poplars converge
on horizons: marching, but art.

Talcy is a village of 223 people
and a 13th-century chateau
where Ronsard courted Cassandra.
The German cyclist is headed there too.
We're all foreign, with time
to stop for this photo.

The two hourglass shapes you see
in the haze are the nuclear
power plant, France of the future.
That's us beside roses and cornfields,
beside ourselves listening
to nothing spread its wings.

Life Drawing

At night, in the Museum Art School,
Men and women whose daily work
Doesn't require hands or eyes
To surrender to such intimacy,
And the instructor passing over us,
And everything around the room
In shadow gathers to intensify
Light on the model's body,
A stranger's, a woman. The charcoal
Starts erratically, almost
Of its own accord, though
We're hardly aware of time
Anymore, hands moving to match
Body part to body whole, nipple
To breast, the long waist to the shadowy
Haunch like a blue whale rising,
Falling back into the feeding dark.

Her eyes are closed. What could she
Be thinking of? Her boundaries shift
Between each taken breath. More sure
Of their universe than we,
The Old Masters drew her as an angel
Descended, walking across the farmyard
Lost not in thought but motion.

Sundays, the men who hang out
At the park love to describe women.
The young men sweep the air

With huge motions, like liars
After hours of no bass
At the County Reservoir, with a wink
To the boy who caught the fish
But doesn't know yet a woman's figure
Matters enough to tell lies.
The old men's hands seem to stutter.
They might be shaping the lost
Map of Thrace—stone house,
Stone wall, a horse nibbling
Grass, clouds from the long neigh.
Hands that labored in stone
Or wood or dirt for years, when
They're about to fly off the wrists,
Vanish into their pockets.

All the postures of flesh blur
In the merciless overhead lights.
The model stretches. She puts on her glasses
And pads naked and noisily around us
Like a silvery carp stranded on a beach
Or water, as it overflows its banks,
Seeking a new shape. She wants to see
Just how we have depicted her.
Then bends to pick up her clothes, and with
Her back to us puts them on slowly,
Bra, panties and a shirt, bluejeans, rubber thongs.
What lay there in a stillness older
Than statues of gods made from clay and spit
Is a teenager in a Rolling Stones t-shirt.

If she could have watched the lumps
Of charcoal careful to reproduce
She might have thought: child
Playing dead at sunset after supper
On the front lawn under the privet;

Horizon, hill; hill after hill
Someone cares enough about
To sit and draw. We all love to look,
And as we can't always touch
We walk home to more familiar shapes.
The curves follow the light
From the open door, and even as I sit
On the bed and stare, and wake her,
Even as my breathing starts to echo hers,
There is something I can't have.
The drowsy neck, the hollow
Back of the knees, the ear that
Goes around, the feet like a slum
At dawn. There is also the body
As a version of habit, skin-deep;
Body going deeper, pleasuring itself
Even as it pleasures us; body the hotel
Of the spirit, elusive and presiding,
Belonging to nothing and to no one.

A House

Their mouths blur like leaves caught
    In a crosswind. Lips barely, softly
Touching there, and behind the lips the hard

    White teeth, and further in, pink membranes
Pulsing to seize a breath. How deep is a mouth?
    How far in before you find the other?

Some nights they fall asleep like that.
    Then wake, walk out to check the weather,
Breakfast together, and off to the world

For a day. All morning and all afternoon
Inside the house shadows change places
    With light. Noon, then twilight, dusk,

Until the shadows become one darkness.
    How thoughtless it looks to a passerby—
Room by room the lamps go on

    As though to repair the harm
The hours have done. But what can you say
    In dark or light that hasn't been said?

Good morning, good night, a kiss again?
    Then, in the body's deepest place—as in a room
Revisited after years away, some space

    You thought of as your own, same radio, same bed
And sink, same view—you meet another
    Passing through, a pilgrim, not quite

Familiar, not quite a stranger. What
    Will you say? *This is where things change,*
Sometimes. This is how some people love.

GREGORY ORR

We Must Make a Kingdom of It

So that a colony will breed here,
love rubs together two words:
"I" and "she." How the long bone
of the personal pronoun
warms its cold length against her fur.

She plants the word "desire"
that makes the very air
amorous, that causes the light,
from its tall stalk, to bend down
until it almost kisses the ground.

It was green, I saw it—tendril
flickering from dry soil
like a grass snake's tongue;
call it "flame"—light
become life, what the word
wants, what the earth
in its turning
yearns for: to writhe and rise up,
even to fly briefly
like the shovelful over
the gravedigger's shoulder.

A Shelf Is a Ledge

I don't understand by what perversity
Darwin and St. Paul are kissing cousins
on my shelf. And how they both lean against
an encyclopedia of history . . .
It must give them bad dreams.
I watch Saul topple from his horse, but
Paul's all right. Darwin in the underbrush
glimpses a finch. And then there's that damned
history book ticking all night
like a cheap clock while it adds
the day's events to its late blank pages
and erases the early ones so it has
more space . . .
               It's true a sane man
would resist the temptation to animate
dead things of the object world, and
such a shunning proves he's sane. Myself,
I hear a blessed humming in my head
and I'm its glad amanuensis.
Paul's taught me this: Love passes
understanding. And Darwin's on my side
as he screams in the dark: Survive! Survive!

The Voyages

It's late when I try to sleep, resting
one hand on your hip, the other on my chest
where the rise and fall of breath
is a faint light that brightens and fades.
Today the doctor placed his stethoscope
against your belly and an amplifier
filled the tiny room with a scene
from old war movies—the submarine,
the churning of a destroyer's engines
fathoms above rapt, terrified sailors.
Child's heart, whose thrumming the doctor
pronounced as perfect as such things
can be guessed across such gulfs.

Here, deep in the night, I calm my fears
by choosing a place among Homer's crew,
lolling on Hades' shore. Inland, Odysseus
brims a trench with blood, extorts predictions
from the thirsty dead. But common sailors
already know that launching and wrecks
make the same sounds: scrape of keel on rock,
loud cries. As for the rest,
we need our ignorance to keep us brave.

ROBERT PACK

Clayfeld's Glove

Clayfeld believed indulging in one's whims
   improved the circulation
of despondent blood; whims, the sculptor in him
   could persuade himself,
counted as a form of inspiration.
   One day, browsing
in a sports equipment store, he noticed how
   the baseball gloves had changed,
how large the webbing had become, and he decided
   he would fly to Arizona
where his mother lived to see if she had stored
   the yellow baseball glove
Clayfeld had oiled and pounded into shape
   when he was still a boy.
"Are you all right?" the salesman asked,
   and Clayfeld knew
he must have blushed to recollect the time
   he'd grabbed his baseball glove
to hide his private parts that night
   his mother, without warning,
walked into his room. He thought maybe he'd sculpt
   a naked statue of himself—
a true artistic first: a baseball glove where once
   a fig leaf would have been.
Clayfeld awoke in Arizona to the smell
   of lamb chops' sizzling,
which his mother served him with his eggs
   just as she used to do
when he was lifting weights to put some muscle
   on his skinny frame.

"Everything I've kept of yours," she said,
   "is packed away in boxes
chronologically and stacked in the garage."
   Shoes, hair clippings, letters,
layer after layer, like excavations
   from an ancient Jericho,
waited to be exhumed—and then, behold!
   he found a baseball glove,
but one too skimpy to have been his own.
   Maybe, he thought, this was
his father's glove; maybe mother had mistaken
   father's glove for his?
Another statue he might sculpt appeared
   in Clayfeld's mind: his father, poised
in naked grandeur, just as Michelangelo
   had once conceived his David,
sling-shot stone in hand, prepared himself
   to backhand any grounder
that might yield the rally-killing double play.
   "I don't know how
this glove could be your father's,"
   Clayfeld's mother scolded him,
and then it all came swirling back to her:
   "You couldn't have been more
than four or five," she said, "that spring your father
   took you out to have a catch
when he had finished with his chores—and I
   mean every single day!
I'd stand there in the doorway shouting
   'Dinner will get spoiled
unless the two of you come in right now!'
   But nothing I could threaten
seemed to do much good. And so one evening
   after you had muddied up
the living room as usual, I boiled the glove,
   piled mashed potatoes

neatly in the pocket, sprinkled it
　　with parsley, squeezed into
my tightest bathing suit, my highest heels,
　　and sashayed in
to score my point." A statue of his mother
　　formed in Clayfeld's mind,
and then Clayfeld recalled his father's words
　　before he tucked him
into bed that night: "From now on, son,
　　we'll have to end
our catch on time." It had begun to rain.
　　He saw the red buds
of the maple tree outside his room
　　reflect his window lamp.
His father handed him a sandwich
　　he had sneaked upstairs
inside his baseball cap. "I'll bet you didn't know
　　that I could cook," he said.
Now in this Arizona noon, those open boxes
　　blazing in the entryway
of the garage, the lines in Clayfeld's mother's face
　　seemed smoothed out by the sun.
"Yes, everything will be put back exactly
　　in its place," he promised her.
But Clayfeld wondered if his grief would ever end.
　　Maybe if he had children
of his own? He thought someday he'd do
　　his father's bust—he'd catch the grim
thrust of his head, like David looking past his shoulder
　　through the empty light,
without his body there to trouble him.

Clayfeld's Twin

"My dear, indulgent, older (by five minutes) brother,"
    Clayfeld's brother wrote,
"despite your psychic warnings, I have had
    another accident—
my perverse way (no doubt you'll think) of wooing
    Mother Nature's preference:
attention-getting is the cruder way
    of putting it, I know.
So be it, then; here are the gruesome facts:
    I caught a fly-hook
(Parmachene Belle, your favorite) in my left eye
    while fishing with (how's this
for a surprise?) Eileen, my neighbor's wife.
    The doctor still has hope,
but I may lose my sight. There's no help you
    can give right now, so save yourself
time and expense; don't bother coming out.
    Her husband stopped by
at the hospital to say a righteous God
    had punished me. 'An eye
for an Eileen,' quoth I, but, break O heart!,
    the bastard missed my pun."
The smudgy letter blurring as he stared,
    Clayfeld almost could hear
his brother's laughter leaping the abyss
    between them—laughter, he imagined,
that, had Cain posssessed it, might have stopped the blow
    that's cursed our whole inheritance.
And yet, a mutilated eye, how could his brother
    laugh that fact away?
Or maybe he was showing off, one more
    bravura boast to demonstrate

he could defy whatever fortune dumped on him,
    as if, although a physicist,
he still required a smirking faith to see
    the quarky universe
of stellar fire-burst or black-hole collapse
    as cosmic comedy.
Clayfeld recalled the day that Bill,
    his sympathetic stepfather,
had his left hand ripped clean off by the combine
    he had worked for years. Could that
have been the origin of Clayfeld's brother's
    proneness to dumb accidents,
the cause, as well, of his disdain for chance?
    Clayfeld remembered Bill
just sat there in the kitchen with his stump
    wrapped in his shirt, waiting
for the ambulance to come. "The kitchen
    needs another coat of paint,"
he joshed, and once again his brother's laugh
    squawked out so coarsely
Clayfeld thought he'd heard the panicked quacking
    of his pet duck, Ishmael,
as if he watched the lunging red fox catch him
    lolling on the muddy shore.
Despite his brother's stricture not to come,
    Clayfeld flew to Los Angeles
to be with him, guessing his stubborn brother
    was too proud to ask, and yet
resenting him for never saying right out
    bluntly what he felt:
"I'm hurt. I'm scared. I need your help!" Why couldn't
    his own brother simply let
those seething, vexed, laughed-down emotions out?
    "Here lies your blinded, *pun*-
ished, *pupil* of romance, and *cornea* than ever,"
    Clayfeld's brother greeted him.

Shocked Clayfeld had no quip to answer back;
    he pressed his cheek against
the good side of his brother's face and wept—
    sobs surged up from his ribs,
he gagged for breath, a salt stream swamped his lips,
    bubbling with mumbled sounds
of garbled words. "He'll be all right. Don't worry,"
    said the young nurse, holding
Clayfeld's shoulders as he shook; "the bandages
    come off tomorrow and you'll see!"
But Clayfeld's weeping was not finished yet.
    Even his twin did not know
he still harbored all those ancient, unshed tears;
    the sobs kept coming on,
contorting him. Why should his brother's laughter
    be the cause? Clayfeld's gasps
lengthened out to lesser heaves; his moaning
    steadied into measured breaths;
for just an instant, like a baby, he dozed off
    upon his brother's chest. It's true
the nurse thought that she heard Clayfeld call for someone—
    "Ishmael"? She asked
"Is that your brother's childhood name for you?"

Clayfeld's Daughter Reveals Her Plans

"A feast of light!" Clayfeld proclaimed
while waiting for his daughter to appear.
    Surveying the horizon
from his own dear hill where he and Evelyn
    had lived for thirty years,
Clayfeld watched sunset orange stream across the field
    beneath the altocumulus
configuration of ribbed clouds that formed
    a vast, arched passageway
which magnified the light by whirling it
    up from the meadow to the clouds
and back again as if such mirroring
    of brazen orange
burnishing itself would never end.
    The clouds then sealed the sun
behind the mountain top; the buried light was gone
    as if a black hole's pull
had sucked it from the valley: Clayfeld let
    a little gasp escape despite
the many times he'd witnessed this same scene.
    Stunned Clayfeld ruminated
he had never seen a sunset end so fast,
    and that, perhaps, accounted
for the gust of calm despondency, like mist
    unfurling on a morning lake,
that wafted through his mind—yes, *calm*, since after
    all these watchful years,
Clayfeld could now take pleasure even
    in his somber autumn moods.
"The whole shebang, from A to Z, one must
    embrace it all!" resounding
Clayfeld sermonized into the sullen dark.
    The clouds had drifted on:

now Capricorn peered down the southern sky
   across the zodiac
as Cynthia arrived, pale and disheveled
   from her long day's drive.
"Mom knows why I've come home to talk to you.
   I'm planning to get married, Dad,
in just one month." "She knows? Your mother knows?"
   astonished Clayfeld blathered
to his starlit daughter at the entryway. "His ancestors rebuilt
   their Maryland estate after
the Civil War, and, like his grandfather,
   he plans to run for Congress."
Sexual congress was the quip that Clayfeld
   managed to suppress.
"I brought a present, Dad," and, for an instant,
   Clayfeld's spirits lightened
as she handed him a box with horses leaping
   neatly over rocky streams.
"And what the hell is this?" demanded Clayfeld's
   disappointed, high-pitched voice.
"A hunting horn, Dad," Cynthia replied,
   "two days before the wedding
there will be a fox hunt for the special guests,
   and you've been honored
to begin it with the blowing of this horn.
   George Washington loved fox hunting,
and Thomas Jefferson, and . . ." "Fox hunting!"
   flushed Clayfeld bellowed out,
"a fucking fox hunt thought up by some sterile,
   syphilitic, lisping English earl
to titillate himself, and you want me
   parading on their lawn
in Mr. Mincing Blueblood's scarlet britches
   and my yarmulke—

or maybe I should wear my baseball cap?—
   tooting my brains away?"
Clayfeld, disconsolate, stamped from the room,
   his wife pursuing him:
"For once you've got to trust what Cynthia
   decides is right for her!"
So on the day assigned, proud Clayfeld stood there
   in his baseball cap, intractable,
defiant, as the umber sun rose up
   behind the humid trees
and spread its haze along the whitewashed fences
   crossing through the field
to the ravine that marked the forest's edge.
   Like one of Joshua's priests,
summoned to Jericho, he lifted up his horn
   and wailed the hollow signal
to the straining dogs to let the hunt commence.
   And then, unheard amid the din,
distracted Clayfeld improvised a little,
   simple, two-note tune—
first one note held, repeating liltingly
   upon a softer, quicker note—
which his true ears alone would understand
   sounded the cadence, Cyn·thi·a,
receding in the unfamiliar dawn
   of silken Maryland.

Clayfeld's Anniversary Song

When the evolutionary biologist J. B. S. Haldane was
asked about the nature of the creator, he replied:
"An inordinate fondness for beetles!"

There's no accounting for
one's taste in love, my dear, even with God.
    Some eighty-five percent
of all animal species comprise insects,
    with an inscrutable
preponderance of beetles! Although they seem
    grotesque to you and me
(Stag males can kill with their huge mandibles
    or seize their choiceless mates)
yet there they are, Nature's elect display,
    with such variety
embellishing a single theme great Bach's
    imagination pales
by comparison. Having invaded
    on water, land and air,
adorers of decay, some woo their mates
    by rubbing their own wings
to rough out strains of ragged melody;
    while some display their fire
(protected by an inner layer of cells
    so they won't burn themselves),
delighting in each other with abandon
    we can't emulate.
A quibble in the cosmic scheme of things,
    no doubt: Nature is not
concerned with individuals, even
    species are cast away—
tonnage of dinosaurs with just a little
    climate shift. Yes, life alone

is what God seems to care about—only
    ongoing life, trying
new forms for His vast, slapdash enterprise
    of changing things. Against
such precedent divine, what arrogance
    is human constancy—
rebellion in the most unnatural
    and prideful way of love
seeking to preserve the past. No wonder
    we're appalled by death,
ashamed of our own sweat, and endlessly
    examining ourselves.
What parents ever wished their child would be
    an evolutionary
breakthrough, rendering us obsolete?
    The quintessential prayer
that dwells in every human heart repeats:
    O, Lord, keep things the same;
let me be me again in paradise,
    reading in my old chair
or strolling through a grove of evergreens.
    I fear that we'll be viewed
by Him as undeserving of the life
    we've got, and punished, yet
no differently than other creatures are—
    we'll be forgotten too,
beetles and all. Who knows—perhaps some day
    He'll tire: "Enough!" He'll cry,
and start a list of everything He's done.
    And when He gets way back
to counting us, and pictures you again,
    just as I see you now—
watering the wilted fuchsia hanging
    beside the limestone wall,

plucking the dead leaves from the zinnias—
   He'll think: "It's not their fault
they measured time in anniversaries
   as if their need for meaning
made me manifest in *their* intent;
   I burdened them with an
excessive will to live. But by my beard,
   my beetles were magnificent!"

JAY PARINI

This Kampuchea

We sit in a *tuk-tuk* with binoculars,
sipping Fantas, as a hot white wind
blows over water half a mile wide;
the heat is nearly what we can't abide:
pale tourists, young voyeurs; we find
humidity a subject. Kids with scars

across their cheeks and narrow backs beg
candies, cigarettes. We give them coins
that mean so little we can hardly not afford
to give them up. Such charity! I pour
my Fanta in a cup and give a swig
to a small boy whose mother joins

us from behind a shack, an improvised
bamboo construction housing refugees.
She hasn't said a word since she escaped,
the doctor tells us. Maybe she was raped
at knife point, maybe she had seen the trees
strung out with villagers Pol Pot despised

for simply being there? Then we all hear
they shot her husband in a ditch before her eyes;
her eyes seem blank now, darkly blank.
I notice that she never seems to blink
but watches like the bald-eyed moon, in fear,
as children utter their unlovely cries

for candy, cigarettes, for sips of Fanta
from my tinny cup. The bamboo clicks
in big-finned leaves across the river where

Cambodia has turned in its despair
to Kampuchea, where the golden bricks
of Ankor Wat sink like Atlantis

into jungle depths, the lost bright heart
of ancient quietude that's since been drowned
in spit and blood. I wonder why we came
to this sad border and if we're to blame
as much as anyone in that swart
jungle where the millions died as Death found

easy entrance on the world, engorged
itself, while faces turned another way.
Lon Nol, Pol Pot, the bloated Princes
whom the Rouge detested: none convinces
us that he's to blame. We'll never say
"this one" or "that" and feel relieved, purged

and guiltless, free to sail by 747
home to seasons in the hills of ease.
This Kampuchea will become a tomb
inside me, alien, but still a home
in some strange way—an altar where my knees
will fall at intervals, an odd chance given

to me as a gift, a place to bow
in obeisance to the darkest gods
who rule the heart whenever we ignore
our greatest charge: to watch and pray. The shore-
line glistens as a boy lets down a bamboo
rod, an old man settles by a tree and nods

off into dreams, a flame-bright bird
sails over water without any sense
of human borders. Children scurry to a jeep
beside us where the spoils are greater, as we keep
to schedule and drive away: untold expense
now memorized behind us, word for word.

The Function of Winter

I'm for it, as the last leaves shred
or powder on the walks, as sparrows find
the driest footing, and November rains
grow hard as salt sprayed over roads.
The circulating spores take cover
where they can, and light runs level
to the ground again: no more the vertical
blond summer sheen that occupies a day
but winter flatness—light as part of things,
not things themselves. My heart's in storage
for the six month siege we're in for here,
laid up for use a little at a time
like hardtack on a polar expedition,
coveted though stale. Ideas, which in
summer hung a crazy jungle in my head,
subside now, separate and gleam in parts;
I braid them for display on winter walls
like garlic tails or onions, crisp bay wreathes.
One by one, I'll pluck them into spring.
If truth be told, I find it easier
to live this way: the fructifying boom
of summer over, wild birds gone, and wind
along the ground where cuffs can feel it.
Everything's in reach or neatly labelled
on my basement shelves. I'm ready to begin
to see what happened when my heart was hot,
my head too dazzled by itself to think.

Skiing Home at Dusk

This is the blessed hour when shadows lenthen
on the bloodlit snow, when skiers mount
the billows with an ease, a forward *shush*,

and memory excites the tilt toward home:
the florid fire that blossoms over logs,
the candle and the book, hibernal harvest.

Motion through the trees collects the soul,
a whispering in transit, wind that's caught
like music in a flute's brief wooden throat.

This is the hour of accepted grace,
when everywhere we've been comes down to this:
the edge of day, where particles of thought

cohere like atoms in a structured dance
around one center that we call ourselves,
like poetry: the patterned perfect dance

of sentences that rise and fall with sense,
a language adequate to what we see
and feel and hear, a broad equivalence,

the center of the mind as clear as winter
with its empty backlit zero sky,
the motes of snow-dust blowing from the trees.

This is the hour when skiers and their skiis
make one crisp sound, when every object
whistles out its name, when *home* is home.

Suburban Swamp

The swamp at the end of our cozy county road
does nothing for the value of what we own;
it's what the agents call an eyesore
and the neighbors never mention to their friends,
half wishing what they never set in words
will not exist. I'm standing by the stumps
that fizzle like antacid tabs in water,
the tatty oaks too old for leaves, loose
at the roots like blackened teeth that wobble
in the gums, a peridontal nightmare.
This was once a lake, old timers say,
remembering the sunny Sunday picnics
where these mossbanks grow or, some say,
"fester." Frogs exhale into the midday air.
The green-gold water pops its blisters.
Winds are redolent of larval scum
that might well be a soothing balm for backache
in an old wives tale if old wives lived.
The Indians came out in bark canoes
two centuries ago; now Boy Scouts tramp
these margins for a merit badge or two,
birdwatchers wait for oddly-feathered friends,
and secret moralists inspect the setting
for its sheer decay. I like it how
what happens happens out of sight here.
Business goes on beneath the surface:
transformations: water into froth,
great hulking logs to pulp and steam.
Here every change is hidden but complete,
all purposes obscured—a skilled dismantling,
de-creation into light and air.

LINDA PASTAN

Overture

This is the way
it begins: the small
sure voice of the woodwind
leads us down a path brocaded
with colored leaves,
deep into a forest
we almost remember.
And though the percussions
have no exact equivalent,
soon we will find ourselves
thinking of weather—
a cold front rumbling in—
or of applause,
not for the self
but for someone we watch
bowing at the edge
of a pond whose waters,
like the cello's
darkest waters, part
letting the melody
slip through. This theme
presents itself so shyly
that when it returns full grown,
though it plucks
the live nerve of recollection
we will hear it
as if for the first time.
Make no mistake, this is only

music, shading with evening
into a minor key.
Whole flocks of birds rush up
spreading their night wings
as the harpist, that angel
who guarded the gates
in strict black, sweeps
her arm from E to G to high C,
and the bowing stranger
lifts his wand, letting
the curtains part.

Suffocation

For RJP

In Chekhov's Three Sisters, everyone
is infected with terminal boredom.
When Irena says her soul is like a locked
piano without a key, I want
to tell her that playing the piano too
the fingers can wander up and down
the scales, going nowhere.
And when the talk leads always back
to Moscow, where she longs to be,
I wish I could remind Olga
of the cold, unyielding streets
where even the ice hardens to the color
of stone. Sitting here, watching
someone I love slowly die,
I see how anguish and boredom
can be married for years,
an ill assorted couple, suffocating
in each other's arms.

I watched Masha at the curtain call, the tears
still streaming down her face
as she moved from one self
to the other through the wall
of applause, a kind of backwards birth.
And I wondered where all that feeling
came from if not some deep pool
where one can be dragged and dragged
beneath the surface but never quite drown.
Russia . . . I thought, Russia . . . a country
my grandfather thought he had escaped from
but which we wore always
like the heavy overcoat in the story
by Gogol, or the overcoat he wrapped me in
one night when the grownups kept on talking,
and I shivered and yawned in an ecstasy
of boredom that made my childhood
seem a vast continent I could only escape from
hidden in a coat, in steerage, and at great risk.

The Death of a Parent

Move to the front
of the line
a voice says, and suddenly
there is nobody
left standing between you
and the world, to take
the first blows
on their shoulders.
This is the place in books
where part one ends, and
part two begins,

and there is no part three.
The slate is wiped
not clean but like a canvas
painted over in white
so that a whole new landscape
must be started,
bits of the old
still showing underneath—
those colors sadness lends
to a certain hour of evening.
Now the line of light
at the horizon
is the hinge between earth
and heaven, only visible
a few moments
as the sun drops
its rusted padlock
into place.

Last Words

Let us consider
last words: Goethe's
"More Light," for instance,
or Gertrude Stein, sly
to the end, asking
"But what is the question?"

Consider the fisherman
caught on the hook
of his own death
who saves
his last words
for the sea.

Consider the miner,
the emblem of earth
on his face,
who curses the earth
as he enters it,
mineshaft or grave.

I have heard the dry sound
leaves make
on their way from the tree,
have felt the cold braille
of snow as it melts
in the hand.

It is almost time
to let the curtain
of darkness down
on the perfect exit,
to say one last time
a few loved names,

or else to go out
in silence
like an anonymous star
whose message,
if there is one,
is light years away.

Shadows

Each night this house sinks into the shadows
under its weight of love and fear and pity.
Each morning it floats up again so lightly
it seems attached to sky instead of earth,
a place where we will always go on living
and there will be no dead to leave behind.

But when we think of whom we've left behind
already in the ever hungry shadows,
even in the morning hum of living
we pause a minute and are filled with pity
for the lovely children of the earth
who run up and down the stairs so lightly

and who weave their careless songs so lightly
through the hedges which they play behind
that the fruits and flowers of the earth
rise up on their stems above the shadows.
Perhaps even an apple can feel pity;
perhaps the lilac wants to go on living.

In this house where we have all been living
we bind the family together lightly
with knots made equally of love and pity
and the knowledge that we'll leave behind
only partial memories, scraps of shadows,
trinkets of our years upon the earth.

I think about my father in the earth
as if it were a room in which he's living,
as if it were a house composed of shadows
where he remembers those he loved not lightly,
where he remembers what he left behind.
He had a great capacity for pity

but told me that I mustn't waste my pity
on him—he'd had his share of life on earth,
and he was happy just to leave behind
daughters of daughters who would go on living.
So he seemed to leave us almost lightly,
closing the curtains which were stitched with shadows.

Always save your pity for the living
who walk the eggshell crust of earth so lightly,
in front of them, behind them, only shadows.

ROBERT PINSKY

Sonnet

Afternoon sun on her back,
calm irregular slap
of water against a dock.

Thin pines clamber
over the hill's top—
nothing to remember,

only the same lake
that keeps making the same
sounds under her cheek

and flashing the same color.
No one to say her name,
no need, no one to praise her—

only the lake's voice, over
and over, to keep it before her.

The Want Bone

The tongue of the waves tolled in the earth's bell.
Blue rippled and soaked in the fire of blue.
The dried mouthbones of a shark in the hot swale
Gaped on nothing but sand on either side.

The bone tasted of nothing and smelled of nothing,
A scalded toothless harp, uncrushed, unstrung.
The joined arcs made the shape of birth and craving
And the welded-open shape kept mouthing O.

Ossified cords held the corners together
In groined spirals pleated like a summer dress.
But where was the limber grin, the gash of pleasure?
Infinitesimal mouths bore it away,

The beach scrubbed and etched and pickled it clean.
But O I love you it sings, my little my country
My food my parent my child I want you my own
My flower my fin my life my lightness my O.

Icicles

A brilliant beard of ice
Hangs from the edge of the roof
Harsh and heavy as glass.
The spikes a child breaks off

Taste of wool and the sun.
In the house, some straw for a bed,
Circled by a little train,
Is the tiny image of God.

The sky is fiery blue,
And a fiery morning light
Burns on the fresh deep snow:
Not one track in the street.

Just as the carols tell
Everything is calm and bright:
The town lying still
Frozen silver and white.

Is only one child awake,
Breaking the crystal chimes?—
Knocking them down with a stick,
Leaving the broken stems.

STANLEY PLUMLY

Against Starlings

1

Their song is almost painful the way it
penetrates the air—above the haze and
level of the fields a thin line drawn. A
wire. Where the birdcall goes to ground. But I'd
stand anyway under the oaks lining
the road and whistle, tireless with chances,
tossing, by the handful, the crushed stone.
All of them answered, none of them came down.
By evening there'd be hundreds filling the
trees past hearing, black along the branches.
They'd go off with the guns like buckshot, black,
filling the sky, falling. I held my ears.
The holes in the air closed quickly, then healed.
Birds were bloodless, like smoke, wind in a field—

2

But not to be confused with the cowbird,
its brown head, its conical sparrow's bill,
nor with the red-wing, which is obvious,
even showy, blood or birthmark, nor with
the boat-tailed grackle—though at dusk, when they
gathered from the north, they were all blackbirds.
They were what the night brought, and the blown leaves,
and the cloud come down in the rain. The ease
of it, the way summer would be ending.
When I found one one morning it was the
color of oil in a pool of water,

bronze, blue-green, still shining. The parts that were
missing were throwaway, breast and belly
and the small ink and eye-ring of the eye—

3

Not to be compared with the last native
wild pigeon, trap shot high in Pike County,
Ohio, the fourth day of spring, nineteen
hundred—thirty years after the harvest
of millions filled the buffalo trains east.
They were, by report, 'the most numerous
bird ever to exist on earth,' what the
Narragansett called *Wuskowhan*, the blue
dove, the wanderer, whose flight is silent.
Not to be compared with the smaller, wild
mourning dove, which haunted the afternoon,
which you heard all day till dark. They
were the sound in my sleep those long naps home,
the last train calling down the line in time—

4

Sometimes, at the far end of a pasture,
the burdock and buckwheat thick as the grass
along the hedgework, you could still find nests,
some fallen, some you had to climb to. They
were a kind of evidence, a kind of
science, sticks, straw, and brilliant bits of glass.
My mother had a hat like that, feathered,
flawed—she'd bought it used. It was intricate
and jewelled, the feathers scuffed like a jay's,
and so stiff you could've carried water.
The millinery species is over.
Those nests had nothing in them. Still, sometimes
I'd wait until the autumn light was gone,
the sky half eggshell, half a starling's wing—

Not to be compared with the fluted voice,
the five phrases in different pitches
of the thrush, the one Whitman heard, and Keats.
Sturnus vulgaris vulgaris—not to
be confused with the soft talk and music,
the voice that calls the spirit from the wood.
Those that stayed the winter sat the chimney
to keep warm, and cried down the snow to fly
against the cold. They were impossible.
They'd be dead before spring, or disappear
into the white air. —Not to be confused
with the black leaves whirling up the windward
side of the house, caught in the chimney smoke,
the higher the more invisible—

                    Black.
I saw them cover the sky over a
building once, and storm an alley. They were
a gathering, whole. Yet on the window
sill, individual, stealing the grain
I put there, they'd almost look at me through
the glass. Something magical, practical.
They'd even graze the ground for what had dropped.
I wished for one to come into the house,
and left the window open just enough.
None ever did. That was another year.
What is to be feared is emptiness and
nothing to fill it. I threw a stone or
I didn't throw a stone is one language—
the vowel is a small leaf on the tongue.

With Stephen in Maine

The huge mammalian rocks in front of the lawn,
domestic between the grass and the low tide—
Stephen has set his boat in one of the pools,
his hand the little god that makes it move.
It is cold, the sky the rough wool and gaberdine
of pictures someone almost talented has painted.
Off and on the sun, then Stephen is wading . . .

Yesterday we saw two gulls shot out of the sky.
One of them drifted into shore, broken, half-eaten,
green with the sea. When I found it this morning
all I could think to do was throw it back. One wing.
Its thin blood spread enough that Stephen is finger-
printed and painted with washing and wiping dry.
Even his boat, at the watermark, is stained.

I lift him, put him up on top of my shoulders.
From here he can watch the deep water pile, turn over.
He says, with wonder, that it looks like the ocean
killing itself. He wants to throw stones, he wants
to see how far his boat can sail, will float.
The mile or more from here to there is an order of color,
pitched white and black and dove- or green-gray, blue,

but far and hurt from where he is seeing.

LAWRENCE RAAB

Familiar Landscapes

I

Morning's sudden and extravagant
green seems to suggest the higher
whiter waves of the air, what moves
through the flurry of these
first leaves, floating and falling
beyond everything I am able to see.
Against that brightness, a flock of blue,
a single yellow iris
creaks on its shaft. How persistently
the eye resists the familiar,
so easily finding itself content
among its accustomed walls,
the expected trees and avenues,
that it fails to see them
and will acknowledge
only what has been changed or lost
or taken away.

2

The mountain darkens with the sky
and the quiet lake
holds onto the light as long as it can.
That's the way we looked at it
one summer. The shadowed lane.
The silence of the house.
Sometimes a few words are all we ask for
and it's too much.

With the tube down your throat
you couldn't talk. "Not to be able
to breathe for yourself," the young doctor
told my father, "that's the worst thing
to take away from anyone."

3

Even the most familiar landscape
opens itself to the moon's cold
inspection, and is changed.
Dreaming all night, waking
early, I'm unable to remember
what appeared essential
only a moment ago, an image
perhaps, or a fact that asked
something of me
just because it was there, now
lost altogether in the day's
advances—this absolute blue
against which the wind displays
these clouds as they drift
and gather, shred,
rise, and are carried away.

The Room

For my mother, Marjorie Young Raab
October 10, 1913 – March 20, 1978

Everything has been arranged too carefully.
The way the eyes are closed, that certainty.
I can see it isn't possible to pretend
that the dead are only sleeping.
The way the hands are folded
we don't have to touch them.

When I touched them I knew it wasn't necessary.
I've watched my wife and daughter sleeping.
I've watched you. No matter how still,
there's an imperceptible trembling
accompanies everything that lives.
It's the way a feather sways, that chance.
It's the cloud on the mirror,
that stain. For a while we imagined
our concerns were yours. Is this blue dress
the one you would have wanted to wear?
And these rings, that silver pin?
Is this the music you especially liked to hear?
But the dead among their flowers
have no preferences, and I think
it must be wrong to pretend otherwise,
if only for my sake, and not now for yours.

Desire and Revenge

A slow fall, a long unwinding—
the Mummy's frayed white tape shredding away
as he shuffles toward us, arms
stretched out, unaccustomed even
to the dimmest candle. The leaves
brought him back, that bitter tea,
and desire, and revenge. You can't
stay dead that long and not want
to get back at someone, and that could be
anybody sitting alone in a tent
or poking around a tomb. So he stumbles out
into the light, the girl screams
and faints. She doesn't realize
she's the one he loved
hundreds of years ago,

when he was really alive. And he won't be able
to convince her now. Every time
he gets those dry fingers
around a throat, you know he's strong
but he's slow, and it seems
to occur to no one just to run away.
But we don't miss the point. It's this
close-up of the girl pressed back
against the sacrificial font, eyes
opening even wider, and then the hero
clutching his torch. And then the inevitable,
followed by a few aimless words
of explanation. As the survivors
gather their things together, the sun
blares down its blessing, and everyone
leaves, half-convinced the dead are still
angry, still in love, and sooner or later
they burn for it, unwilling
to lie down quietly, as we know
they should, and let us go.

This Day

Watching the beautiful
sticks of trees as they click and sway,
the first green unravelling,

it's easy to imagine I might
remember this day forever.
I say it to myself,

never to others, while the poem
made hoping to preserve it
is changed, then changed again

to fit another order
it happens to discover.
At the end I find myself

in a room by a window, or at the edge
of a field, with the same clear
sky above me wherein later

I will imagine clouds, as if
some movement were required. That,
or a different kind of stillness.

So there must also be
a family circled round
the bedside of someone

who is dying. I place
myself among them.
All of us are waiting

for the little we believe we need
to hold on to and repeat.
But this is not my family

although it is you
who are dying, your words
I am again unable to imagine

as everything continues
sliding together in the light,
that day so easily

changed to this one,
the sky that is so blue, and the clouds
that cross my gaze with such terrible speed.

IRA SADOFF

Why We Always Take Vacations by the Water

For too long I've watched the ski boat scan
the water the way a gull might pan for fish.
What's a ski boat? I don't know
exactly, and I've never heard of one
discussed on those dogged New England wharfs.

But the boat has spindly legs
that keep its frame from touching ocean
like a reluctant swimmer: my mother
on vacation. What was she doing there
by herself while men read at poolside?

My father must have been long gone, writing
the signs of his legible desire: one love letter
after the next. All his girl friends, I think,
were waiting to have something written
on their faces: waves and lines and furrows,

scrutable maps of where they'd been.
The body had already taken its toll
on my mother—even then I remember wanting
some middle-aged man to appreciate her
the way I did, only more so. I don't love her

that way, though I still have feelings I can't name.
Did I talk about the noise it makes, the boat
with "foils," "ailerons," the puttering machine
like a nagging voice in a cinder block motel?
I often wonder why he left. Too often. Why my wife

and I fight over where to take our one week off
every year and we're still here. None of us can swim.
That's a helpless feeling, like speaking for your parents
when they were far from here twenty years ago.
How did I get from there to here? My confusion

brought me, a silly vehicle I've never seen before
that caught my eye, and a handsome man
in a yachting cap waving from its stern—
he's saying something to my mother we can't hear
as she lets her body slip into the ocean, almost bare.

She doesn't wear a bathing cap, my father notices
her hair spreads on the surface of the water
like a skirt blown upward in a sudden wind.
It maddens us, the passage from a swimming pool
to an unknown boat, a stranger at the helm.

Nazis

Thank God they're all gone
except for one or two in Clinton Maine
who come home from work
at Scott Paper or Diamond Match
to make a few crank calls
to the only Jew in New England
they can find

These make-shift students of history
whose catalogues of facts include
every Jew who gave a dollar
to elect the current governor
every Jew who'd sell this country out
to the insatiable Israeli state

I know exactly how they feel
when they say they want to smash my face

Someone's cheated them
they want to know who it is
they want to know who makes them beg
It's true Let's Be Fair
it's tough for almost everyone
I exaggerate the facts
to make a point

Just when I thought I could walk to the market
just when Jean the checkout girl
asks me how many cords of wood I chopped
and wishes me a Happy Easter
as if I've lived here all my life

Just when I can walk into the bank
and nod at the tellers who know my name
where I work who lived in my house in 1832
who know to the penny the amount
of my tiny Jewish bank account

Just when I'm sure we can all live together
and I can dine in their saltbox dining rooms
with the melancholy painting of Christ
on the wall their only consolation
just when I can borrow my neighbor's ladder
to repair one of the holes in my roof

I pick up the phone
and listen to my instructions

I see the town now from the right perspective
the gunner in the glass bubble

of his fighter plane shadowing the tiny man
with the shopping bag and pointy nose
his overcoat two sizes too large for him
skulking from one doorway to the next
trying to make his own way home

I can see he's not one of us

Mood Indigo

I've tried to trace the reverie
I know is sourceless. Why I love
that shade of blue the veins become
when you press a thumb against my wrist.
Why I take the sighting of the bunting
weighing down the branch of pine
as a sign it's lost, looking for its mate.
Why I think of nineteen forty-two,
the argument before my birth, the torn
evening gown worth nothing now:
it should have warned my mother
how the future held her
like the violent blue of storm
that might break the sky in two.
Like a tablet dropped into
a glass of water, this mood
dissolves and bubbles up a murky brew
of hurt and anger misconstrued.
The color of a bruise, a child before
he draws his first traumatic breath.
Why put a stop to it? Because the hook
of waking in the dark drags me
to the stove's hot pilot light

so I can blow the candle out
to stop the ruse of cheerfulness.
Because I must consume the cold sublime,
the bowl of plums that calls us to the table.

Memorial Days

For Yvette and Robert Sadoff

Whirlwind with a vacuum at four a.m.,
mother always closed the blinds
so neighbors wouldn't know her business.
I never knew what occupied that frenzied mind,
but she kept our house clean and dark,
so we lost day and night. And morning light
we found intrusive as a visit from my busy father.

In his absence she often called me *Robert*,
though the word I thought I heard meant *thief*.
I wasn't sure what I stole from her but rest.
I'd wake her from my many nightmares
before she'd soothe me back to sleep
with a washcloth and a kiss. Near dawn, disheveled,
short of breath, while the TV hissed,

she'd dissolve an aspirin on her tongue, doze off
on our broken down couch. But not before
she made the mirrors clear, dispersed the dust
off old photographs. Her brass ballet slippers
waxed bright in midday light, or was it dusk
before her rags wiped clean those memories?
No complaints, she'd say, or *keep them to yourself.*

She acted hers out like a mime. Just as formerly
she'd stretch before a full-length mirror
and spin her dizzy pirouettes toward the future,
her accompanist, my father. And where was he
on this grieving holiday? She said simply
Men cannot be counted on. Because he worked
too hard at night, he drove away, was driven

to and by the world he found so glamorous.
Perhaps, in such a spotless home, he found no place to sit.
I remember, it was Monday and I didn't have to leave
for school. I woke and thought I heard my mother's heart
beating like a bat beneath an eave. I tiptoed to
her makeshift bed. Covered by a sheet,
she scared me into thinking she was dead.

Since I couldn't face my nightmares, I drew
the blinds and let the light warm her forehead,
erase the dark while I searched out her pulse.
My hand on hers startled her awake. She called me
by my father's name, on a day I can't forget.
Memorial day. The day we're called on to recall
with love the living and the living dead.

CHARLES SIMIC

Against Whatever It Is That's Encroaching

Best of all is to be idle,
And especially on a Thursday,
And to sip wine while studying the light:
The way it ages, yellows, turns ashen
And then hesitates forever
On the threshold of the night
That could be bringing the first frost.

It's good to have a woman around just then,
And two is even better.
Let them whisper to each other
And eye you with a smirk.
Let them roll up their sleeves and unbotton
        their shirts a bit
As this fine old twilight deserves,

And the small schoolboy
Who has come home to a room almost dark
And now watches wide-eyed
The grownups raise their glasses to him,
The giddy-headed, red-haired woman
With eyes tightly shut,
As if she were about to cry or sing.

Ancient Autumn

Is that foolish youth still sawing
The good branch he's sitting on?
Do the orchard and hill wheeze because of it,
And the few remaining apples sway?
Can he see the village and the valley
The way a chicken hawk would?

Already wood-smoke scatters its pale plumes;
The days are getting short and chilly.
Even he must rest from time to time,
So he's lit a long-stemmed pipe
And watches a chimney-sweep at work,
And a woman pin diapers on the line
And then go behind some bushes,
Hike her skirt so that a bit of whiteness shows,
While on the commons, humpbacked men
Roll a barrel of hard cider or beer—
And still beyond, past grazing sheep
Children play soldiers and march in step.

He figures, if the wind changes direction
He'll hear their crisp commands—
But it doesn't, so the black horseman
On the cobble of the road remains inaudible.
One instant he seems to be coming,
In the next to be leaving forever . . .

It's these dumbshows with their vague lessons
That make him thoughtful and melancholy.
He's not even aware that he has resumed sawing,
That the big red sun is beginning to set.

Window Washer

And again the screech of the scaffold
High up there where all our thoughts converge:
Lightheaded, hung
By a leather strap,

Twenty stories up
In the chill of late November
Wiping the grime
Off the pane, the many windows

Which have no way of opening,
Tinted windows mirroring the clouds
That are like equestrian statues,
Phantom liberators with sabers raised

Before these dark offices,
And their anonymous multitudes
Bent over this day's
Wondrously useless labor.

October Arriving

I only have a measly ant
To think with today.
Others have pictures of saints,
Others have clouds in the sky.

The winter might be at the door,
For he's all alone
And in a hurry to hide,
Nevertheless, unable to decide

He retraces his steps
Several times and finds himself
On a huge blank wall
That has no window.

Dark masses of trees outside
Casting their mazes
Only to erase them next
With a sly sea-surging sound.

JIM SIMMERMAN

Child's Grave, Hale County, Alabama

Someone drove a two-by-four
through the heart of this hard land
that even in a good year
will notch a plow blade worthless,
snap the head off a shovel,
or bow a stubborn back.
He'd have had to steal
the wood from a local mill
or steal, by starlight, across
his landlord's farm, to worry
a fencepost out of its well
and lug it the three miles home.
He'd have had to leave his wife
asleep on a corn shuck mat,
leave his broken brogans
by the stove, to slip outside,
quiet as sin, with the child
bundled in a burlap sack.
What a thing to have to do
on a cold night in December,
1936, alone
but for a raspy wind
and the red, rock-ridden dirt
things come down to in the end.
Whoever it was pounded
this shabby half-cross
into the ground must have toiled
all night to root it so:
five feet buried with the child
for the foot of it that shows.

And as there are no words
carved here, it's likely that
the man was illiterate,
or addled with fatigue,
or wrenched simple-minded
by the one simple fact.
Or else the unscored lumber
driven deep into the land
and the hump of busted rock
spoke too plainly of his grief:
forty years layed by and still
there are no words for this.

Hide-and-Go-Seek

Friends forget. I am my own friend for a while:
A child reciting numbers to a tree.
Others leave. The others are not here.

I cannot find them, no matter how I stare
Into each face of every face I dream.
They hide themselves inside themselves. They disappear.

I call their names. Their names drift back to me
Like ripples on a lake before it clears.
Friends forget. It is my own voice I hear.

I cannot keep them, cannot . . . See
How they scatter like leaves in a breeze?
Reflected in a lake, the tree is bare.

Others leave. I think they must forget
The child whose recitations root him here.
He is my friend. We walk together for a while.

For a while we walk together by a lake
where faces swirl like leaves, then disappear.
Their common voice drifts out into the night:

You left   forgot   are not here

Whatever It Is

Near the end we will travel as two old men
Leaning lightly on one another for support—
One of us gone a little milky-eyed,
The other a little deaf.

We'll pack what we need in a cheap valise,
Taking turns so it will not be heavy.
When one of us tires, we'll stop awhile
And build a small fire to warm our hands.

You will have then to describe to me
The woods' deep green, the cobalt sky.
I will point you where the nighthawk calls
So that you see what I hear, so we know . . .

Whatever it is we must come to,
We'll have traveled toward togther.
And when we are led apart at the last
Something of each will go with the other.

Two old men hunched to the curve of the world
And biding a little time between them—
Here is my shoulder steadied for you
Though it was long ago we began the journey.

DAVE SMITH

Cooking Eggs

Museless, parodic new man, how did I come down
to this pitiful squeak?
I'm alone and clenched in the smoky kitchen.
Awkwardly aproned, uncertain,
I try to remember how much butter's enough
to sizzle your pan right,
but the unforgettable rituals of preparation
I didn't watch, the heat
unnerves me now: I'm confused about seasonings,
timing, the small feet
I don't hear on our floor anymore. The bed's
made, the cat's slipped
into the world and dearest wonder you're
gone, your gown only gauze
on a hook. I'm trying to crack a shell cleanly,
thinking how you began it,
that easy, fine-pearly sliding-forth ooze
you'd sing up with no hands
almost, awake or asleep. The simple spurt thickens
fast into pinkish fingers
that wrinkle then swell, fissures of flesh quick
changing to bruises, blisters,
a family of small scars, and that sneaky glaucoma
spreading over the heart.
How can I help broken gold at my hand, the smell
of your breastfalling hair,
which isn't with me anymore? I should have written
out what you did like a poem.

Each knob I touch is too much or not enough so
my butt sags in a puddle
of instant coffee, heaps of waste accuse, mornings
spin due bills, the phone
rings, the dog howls, I listen to a soap's lovers.
That's why I say screw it
and abandon myself to the viciously cold shower.
But when I step forth
there's no towel, just me shivering, naked man
in my mortgaged hunger,
squawking like the cardinal we watched spring by
spring, a grandfather.
He's back, red hot, crooning, holding his limb.
She's at work in the yard,
vacuuming the old dirt for a worm, staying in sight.
Indifferent to eggs now,
she lets him sing on but still struts and flutters.
Or flies off in the sun.
Then he sings louder, as if in fear of winters with
only himself, reaching inside
for new notes: "You wouldn't know me, a better bird
by the hour! Come back.
What do you want? I'm cleaning, cooking. I'm hungry."

It's always been nineteen something for me.
Nineteen for my father all his life,
nineteen for my grandmother who went,
nineteen for my sister who wanders,
nineteen for grandfathers who won't make it,
nineteen for my wife who will, our children,
and, for all I know, yours, and theirs.
Nineteen is a lot of sad, dirty numbers
and something that reports to none of us.

What good are words in the face of numbers?
They keep the shadow under a boat rotting
where I crawled as a child, they hide
the pitted spoon of dreams, they deliver
wind in tunes over the reed-heads of home.
They turn my father's face to a thin plank
where I cross the creek over fallen stars.
They are the zeroes of sorrow something says.

I want to pick up my ears like a tired dog
when the whistling comes over the fences.
I want to lie down and dream of God counting
my sins until in anger he sounds sexual
as a Peterson diesel in a fishing scow.
I want to watch the words: nineteen something.
They'll loop out of sight like a slow worm
and I won't even try to read the slime,
the dirt, or the revolutions of the moon.

A Pinto Mare

Mud packing her gullet the robbin pecks
at winter-withered grass, black eye
cocked, feckless as a man I saw bent
at a radar screen's blipless blue. His
lips spread on a mouthfull of pizza
as the end of the world settles, a joke
I took home when my duty was done. Now

just beyond my window the thunder booms
spring at this scruffy, fearless bird.
There's no worm and no nest in sight—
what makes her keep on, rain misting
through trees slick as missiles? She
rips, skips, takes hunks of the earth,
a nerve dutifully alert to what day is.

Years ago, just married, I walked with
sun fire-tonguing a field's face where
tinfoil the landlord hung flashed out
against crows, a sound like dim swords.
The robins worked, humorless legions
of fathers, mothers, barely lifting
themselves from shadow to shadow and I

found the pinto mare with the half-born
foal: its black, dirt-clotted nostrils,
the short-haired head all night bobbing,
unable to bring its body forth. I thought
Christ, the son of bitch landlord again,
asleep, drunk, his unattended toys blown
into death, drifting without a sound.

Across the pasture the stud's big head
pumped up and down, broad ass scratching
a post as he watched us. Gimpy himself,
he turned away, trotted to deeper green,
one muzzle-muffled snort smart in the air.
Rage? What could he do, or me, or you?
Phantom F-4s from Langley shot overhead.

I wanted to throw rocks, shout, to fist
the sky with anger. Head-down the robins
patiently worked the mud, so I put one
hand on the leathery cheek of the foal
and the other on the pinto's warm rump.
That black eye stuck open, fly-specked,
gleamed when I squatted to look inside.

The past? The future? A small mistake made
in breeding?—I wanted to ask, but the mare
stepped on, head just above the grass-tips,
hunching, trying to eat. Robins waddled in
her rank wake. I heard her teeth grinding
the small-skull rocks, indifferent to me,
as her spittle cut dirt, chewing the sun.

At Frost's Grave

Rain long and abrasive thickens the beard of summer
in Bennington's valley, hiding the bullet-hued
slabs of fieldstone, the sodden tree trunks'
volleys of wind crack down at last to a man's
length in the secret weed and moss-cleft. Looming
at a farmhouse window, a man feels his unshaven
face like a soldier outflanked, waiting now,
and the far mountain's dark ridge comes or goes
in rain like hunger or fear. He tries to remember.
The spatter of so much running water is violent
with sadness but he feels he lacks nothing, wants
only to remember a path walked long ago, light
sudden as sniper-fire, sweetness of logs burning.
For a while he waits, imagining what will happen.
He will take the meadow, somewhere stand foolish,
very still, observing a feather of rising smoke
that might be the flesh-char of a wounded boy's leg.
A spruce or pine points like an oil-soaked torch.
The elms look diseased like the future. In rain
you can't hear or smell and so you must wait.
That is why he is able to see the distant trunk,
enormous and malignant with age, thrashed once
with gusts, to see the goldfinches thrown out
like yellow words against the storm, then each
returned as if summoned, lodged in that darkness.
Later, he will stand there and drift as they do,
with no thought that someone may be watching him,
grateful for rain that washes his steps from earth.

WILLIAM STAFFORD

Burning a Book

Protecting each other, right in the center
a few pages glow a long time.
The cover goes first, then outer leaves
curling away, then spine and a scattering.
Truth, brittle and faint, burns easily,
its fire as hot as the fire lies make—
flame doesn't care. You can usually find
a few charred words in the ashes.

And some books ought to burn, trying for character
but just faking it. More disturbing
than book ashes are whole libraries that no one
got around to writing—desolate
towns, miles of unthought in cities,
and the terrorized countryside where wild dogs
own anything that moves. If a book
isn't written, no one needs to burn it—
ignorance can dance in the absence of fire.

So I've burned books. And there are many
I haven't even written, and nobody has.

Coming to Know

A balloon ascends on that path it finds in the air
fated for it before the world began,
and my eyes following find what they have to find
because they are here and wide and helplessly mine.
A face on the side of that balloon not yet alive
leers forth at what it intends, later,
to know. My face hides, afraid of knowing
too soon that revelation in the expanse of the sky:—

My father's face, dawning in that of his son,
alert, fierce enough to survive, but soft
enough to learn in time how balloons will rise
inevitable, stronger than steel, firm on their path
exactly where Now becomes itself, printed
on a face in the sky, and here like this in a man.

Pilgrims

They come to the door, usually carrying or leading
a child, always with The Book held between them
and the world. They quote Ezekiel, Daniel, Kings.
They look at us and think of Nebuchadnezzar
eating the grass. It is good to listen, because
maybe they are angels, and behind them the sky arches,
the trees glisten in worship of the sun.

These travelers in The Word and their offspring have
their commission from somewhere, filtered down, through
mistakes, pride, greed, and the plans committees
make, the way pilgrims have always come.
Over their shoulders day extends its hand;
beside them a child whimpers. It bows its head
as we bow: it hungers; it cries; it will be fed.

278   WILLIAM STAFFORD

Childish Things

When they light the candles a little propellor
turns the angels around and around.

They are of gold, of thin metal,
with a trumpet held in front of each mouth,

And a sound that comes when a tiny chain
drags across a silvery chime.

Flecks of light dance on the ceiling
from figures that gleam as they pass the flame.

That sight, that sound, that warm candle
shine through the years. You look out the window:

What are you doing with the years that shine
around and around when the angels come?

GEORGE STARBUCK

Songs for the Old New Jersey Shelling the Shouf

Spads Krags battleships howitzers those were the good old days.
   Bangeloring the barbed wire. Setting ablaze
Armored patrols of jack-in-the-boxes, watching the contents pop
   Up and go galloping, writhe, crackle and stop.
And then the good old sing-along at the Malmédy canteen,
Oasis in a no-man's-land of corpses turning green,
Where the booze was booze, and the basketcases gathered in a ring
To join the whores and orderlies and corporals and sing:

"Pikes dirks falchionets scatterguns those were the good old days.
To see the man that strangles you. To see the bastard's gaze
   Intensify, go desperate, and glaze.
And the grapeshot and the cavalry exploding through the haze.
Damn, Sacrebleu, Zounds, Teufel but wasn't that the nuts:
Sticking a pig of a Gascon in his piggery of guts
And trooping all off later to be brave inebriates
And sing the soldier ballad while you drain the Malmsey butts:

"Brands rams javelins catapults cauldrons of boiling oil.
Crosses against the infidel. Alhambras to despoil.
Whole citadels escorted to a torchlight Exodus.
   Whole tribes, Hey Nonny Nonny with a heinousness
   Unparalleled since Darius's days
Those were the winds of widowmaking *those* were the fields of praise
When war was fucking war by fucking Christ and men were men
And dawn still found us caroling and singing once again:

"Rocks prods mastadon-mandibles those were the good old days.
   Heads to be bashed, liver-and-lights to braise

And pass among the warriors in order of blood rank
Before the commonality of merrymakers drank
The bloodred blood of victory and chug-a-lugged along
   Beside the ancient chieftain's dance and song:

"Kicks to the jaw! Knees to the testicles! Teeth to the jugular!"—
The song of how it used to be before the forests were
   Brought down and the great god took up the club
   And rucksack of the churl Beelzebub.

Hardearned Overturned Caribbean Basin Stomp

     Gorgeously the *QE2* invaded Grenada.
     Blazing away like Xmas. Broads and booze!
     Fragments of a big brass figurehead, guess whose,
     Lashed to the yardarm. Yankeedom had made a

     Deal! Send me your Derek Walcotts your Vada
     Pinsons your Harry Belafontes and your Rod Carews—
     Quid pro quo for the juiced-up jet-set refuse,
     The ruck of Uncle Slambam's neatsy nephews
     I dump on your quaint ancient quays and queues.

     Deal! lady with a ganja lemonade a
     Grade-A grenadine grog and a contac fuse.
     Deal! player-to-be-named-later in the Orlando Cepeda
     Marianne Moore Bob Vesco Howard Hughes
     Meganegotiation. Whatcha fraida?
     Liberty-gibbet she loaded. Send canoes.

The New Republic Is Infuriated
at the News Coverage

Teletype-music. OK, Maestro, hit it.
Chug chug chug chug chug, but the way they've split it
Into its drumbeats and re-edited it it
Dances like a machine-gun. Like a bird.

Two sentences. Ten seconds of Mirages.
The fashionable condos on the plages
Precipitated into their garages
Like slats into a trash can. Now this word.

The roteness. That's what gravels Marty Peretz.
Some namby-pamby in a trenchcoat ferrets
Out a Mirage'd size-seven and that's Eretz
Israel. That's the wrap-up. That's absurd.
Bittabup bittabeep bittaboop it's . . . Anchornerd

And a ten-second summing-up commences.
The policy of state and its defenses
Shall go the way of last year's Lech Walesas:
Flashcard among a thousand bright unblurred
Experiences to be monitored

To jazz, when we have crisply disinterred
The Year That Was on January third.
No wonder Marty flares and Marty winces.
No wonder he says nothing that convinces
The cameras to backtrack. Now this word.

GERALD STERN

I Sometimes Think of the Lamb

I sometimes think of the lamb when I crawl down
my flight of stairs, my back is twisted sideways
in a great arc of pain from the shoulder down
and the buttocks up. I think of the lamb through my tears
as I go down a step at a time, my left hand
squeezing the rail, my right hand holding my thigh
and lifting it up. As long as there is a lamb
I can get on my hands and knees if I have to
and walk across the floor like a limp wolf,
and I can get my body to the sink
and lift myself up to the white porcelain.
As long as there is a lamb, as long as he lives
in his brown pen or his green meadow,
as long as he kneels on the platform staring at the light,
surrounded by men and women with raised fingers,
as long as he has that little hump on his rear
and that little curve to his tail, as long as his foot
steps over the edge in terror and ignorance,
as long as he holds a cup to his own side,
as long as he is stabbed and venerated,
as long as there are hooves—and clattering—
as long as there is screaming and butchering.

The Dog

What I was doing with my white teeth exposed
like that on the side of the road I don't know,
and I don't know why I lay beside the sewer
so that lover of dead things could come back
with his pencil sharpened and his piece of white paper.
I was there for a good two hours whistling
dirges, shrieking a little, terrifying
hearts with my whimpering cries before I died
by pulling the one leg up and stiffening.
There is a look we have with the hair of the chin
curled in mid-air, there is a look with the belly
stopped in the midst of its greed. The lover of dead things
stoops to feel me, his hand is shaking. I know
his mouth is open and his glasses are slipping.
I think his pencil must be jerking and the terror
of smell—and sight—is overtaking him;
I know he has that terrified faraway look
that death brings—he is contemplating. I want him
to touch my forehead once and rub my muzzle
before he lifts me up and throws me into
that little valley. I hope he doesn't use
his shoe for fear of touching me; I know,
or used to know, the grasses down there; I think
I knew a hundred smells. I hope the dog's way
doesn't overtake him, one quick push,
barely that, and the mind freed, something else,
some other thing, to take its place. Great heart,
great human heart, keep loving me as you lift me,
give me your tears, great loving stranger, remember
the death of dogs, forgive the yapping, forgive
the shitting, let there be pity, give me your pity.
How could there be enough? I have given
my life for this, emotion has ruined me, oh lover,

I have exchanged my wildness—little tricks
with the mouth and feet, with the tail, my tongue is a parrot's,
I am a rampant horse, I am a lion,
I wait for the cookie, I snap my teeth—
as you have taught me, oh distant and brilliant and lonely.

This Was a Wonderful Night

This was a wonderful night. I heard the Brahms
piano quintet, I read a poem by Schiller,
I read a story, I listened to *Gloomy Sunday*.
No-one called me, I studied the birthday poem
of Alvaro de Campos. I thought, if there was time,
I'd think of my garden—all that lettuce, wasted,
all those huge tomatoes lying on the ground
rotting, and I'd think of the sticks I put there,
waving goodbye, those bearded sticks. De Campos,
he was the one who suffered most, his birthday
was like a knife to him; he sat in a chair
remembering his aunts; he thought of the flowers
and cakes, he thought of the sideboard crowded with gifts.
I look at the photo of Billie Holiday;
I turn the light bulb on and off. I envy
those poets who loved their childhood, those who remember
the extra places laid out, the china and glasses.
They want to devour the past, they revel in pity,
they live like burnt-out matches, memory ruins them;
again and again they go back to the first place.
De Campos and I are sitting on a bench
in some American city. He hardly knows
how much I love his country. I have two things
to tell him about my childhood, one is the ice
on top of the milk, one is the card in the window—

three things—the smell of coal. There is some snow
left on the street, the wind is blowing. He trembles
and touches the buttons on his vest. His house
is gone, his aunts are dead, the tears run down
our cheeks and chins, we are like babies, crying.
"Leave thinking to the head," he says. I sob,
"I don't have birthdays any more," I say,
I just go on," although I hardly feel
the sadness, there is such joy in being there
on that small bench, watching the sycamores,
looking for birds in the snow, listening for boots,
staring at the begonias, getting up
and down to rub the leaves and touch the buds—
endless pleasure, talking about New York,
comparing pain, writing the names down
of all the cities south of Lisbon, singing
one or two songs—a hundred years for him,
a little less for me, going east and west
in the new country, my heart forever pounding.

ANNE STEVENSON

Hands

Made up in death as never in life,
mother's face was a mask
set in museum satin.

But her hands. In her hands,
resting not crossing on her paisley dress
(deep combs of her pores,

her windfall palms, familiar routes
on maps not entirely hers
in those stifling flowers) lay

a great many shards of lost hours
with her growing children. As when,
tossing my bike

on the greypainted backyard stairs,
I pitched myself up, through the screen door
arguing with my sister, 'Me? Marry?

Never! Unless I can marry a genius.'
I was in love with Mr. Wullover,
a pianist.

Mother's hands moved *staccato* on a fat ham
she was pricking with cloves.
'You'll be lucky, I'd say, to marry a kind man.'

I was aghast.
If you couldn't *be* a genius, at least
you could marry one. How else would you last?

My sister was conspiring to marry her violin teacher.
Why shouldn't I marry a piano
in Mr. Wullover?

As it turned out, Mr. Wullover died
ten years before my mother.
Suicide on the eve of his wedding, O, to another.

No one said much about why at home. At school
Jenny told me in her Frankenstein whisper,
"He was gay!"

Gay? And wasn't it a good loving thing
to be gay? As good as to be kind
I thought then,

and said as much to my silent mother
as she wrung out a cloth until her knuckles shone,
white bone under raw thin skin.

Shale

For Roger Garfitt

that comes to pieces in your hand
like stale biscuit; birth book
how many million years
left out in the rain. Break back

the pages, the flaking pages
to reveal our own hairline habitations,
the airless museum in which we're
still chained into that still ocean,

while all this burly and stirring water—
motion in monotonous repetition—
washes with silt our Jarassic numbness,
the shelves of ourselves to which we will not return.

Bedded in shale, in its negative evidence,
this Venus shell is small as maybe she was.
The fan-shaped tracery of vertical ridges
could be fine-spread, radiant hair,

or proof of what we take to be
her temper—hot sluttishness loosened
by accident into cold mudslide,
preserving a hated symmetry, a hated elegance.

There is so little sheltered, kept, little
and frail, broken in excavation, half
buried, half broken, poor real child in the boulder
that finds the right shape of its mind

only at the moment of disintegration.
And yet—this clear cuniform in rock;
this sea urchin humping its flower under
'low flying phantoms' . . . this flowing anemone.

MARK STRAND

Always

For Charles Simic

Always so late in the day
in their rumpled clothes, sitting
around a table lit by a single bulb,
the great forgetters were hard at work.
They tilted their heads to one side, closing their eyes.
Then a house disappeared and a man in his yard
with all his flowers in a row.
The moon was next to go.
The great forgetters wrinkled their brows.
Then Florida went and San Francisco
where tugs and barges leave
small gleaming scars across the Bay.
One of the great forgetters struck a match.
Gone were the harps of beaded lights
that vault the rivers of New York.
Another filled his glass
and that was it for crowds at evening
under sulphur yellow streetlamps coming on.
And afterwards Bulgaria was gone, and then Japan.
'Where will it end?' one of them said.
'Such difficult work, pursuing the fate
of everything known,' said another.
'Yes,' said a third, 'down to the last stone,
and only the cold zero of perfection
left for the imagination.'
The great forgetters slouched in their chairs.
Suddenly Asia was gone, and the evening star,

and the common sorrows of the sun.
One of them yawned. Another coughed.
The last one gazed at the window:
not a cloud, not a tree,
the blaze of promise everywhere.

The Continental College of Beauty

For Nolan Miller

The city was flooded with light
that burrowed through mist and morning cloud-cover,
giving the lordly rivers their samite robes.
Out to The Narrows the weather was all arranged.
Tugs, gilded and sleek, in the harbour were stitching the glitter
and graveyard grass, littered with bottles and ash,
glowed as it did in pure wilderness days.
Down in the subway, somebody said,
'Longing is turned into fullness transparent as sunlight.'
Everyone clapped and rose to street-level where the blaze
of tenement windows, of storefront glass was blinding.
This was the time of angelic surprise, of impalpable chance.
Baskets of pears, boxes of plums, racks of oranges gleamed.
Counters of cheese, aisles of meat went pink in the glare.
The shawls of the poor were suddenly mended, the glazed
faces of sleepers rose from the pitch of their personal lives.
The Continental College of Beauty had opened its doors.

For a minute no one would die.
Each eye was a window through which an invisible energy poured
and the flash and flare of truth leapt from the language
that mourned for itself the night before.
Words of the bright mid-morning had risen
into the fuming air. Somebody climbing the steps to his house

looked to the city and said, 'A great similitude spans all.'
And somebody else looked up from her book that sang
the unguarded night of stars and saw that the moon,
stone pillow of angels, had gone, and saw nothing but lustre
washing the streets, and stacks of fuel-fed roses
burning at the city's edge. The armies
of students and drifters that had circled the globe for years
heard a voice from a radio buried in leaves
say that the prose of everyday life was turning to gold.

Over crescents of worried water
flotillas of swans, unaging, paddled
and in the park's tall elms desire flared.
A man raking leaves, who knew he was dying said,
'The wind of heaven wheels round and everything shines.'
The flags of sorrow had been shredded by furious gusts.
Bones long stiffened under the gowns love wore, a woman's
oval face, an old man's golden hair, glowed in the fabulous instant.
And the girl was freed who grieved windswept guitars,
O heart, unwedded, on lonely shores. The rain's monotonous pounding
had come to an end. It was a day of glory wherever you were.
The wind was in flames, was everywhere circling the towers,
the high glass houses, the streaming halls, the painted floors.
Even the fields of sleep were filled with fire
because suddenly out of the blue
the Continental College of Beauty had opened its doors.

Franz

It was the middle of the night.
The beauty parlors were closed and the pale moon
Raced above the water towers.
"Franz," screamed the woman, "take the corpse outside;
It's impossible to think in here."

"Yes, Ma'm," said the hunchback. When she was alone
She undid the top two buttons
Of her blouse, crossed the room and played
The upright in the corner there.
The brief arrangements of her feeling—flawless—
Bloomed in the October chill.
Cold roses filled the rooms upstairs. Franz,
Who stood beside the corpse, closed
His eyes and breathed the scented air. If only
He could have such pleasure every night,
If only the amazing speech of love were not
So frail and could be caught and held
Forever. Poor Franz. Time was always
Spinning out of reach. The dark
Trees swayed above the bending blades of grass.
A neighbor's dog, across whose back
Small dots of shadow strayed, had come to sniff
The dead man's matted hair. Far off,
The last commuter train whizzed past. Franz
Stared for a moment at the dog,
Then quickly checked his watch. It was getting late.
It was cold. His back was tired. Then
the music stopped and the lights inside the house
Went out. There was a crouching stillness
Everywhere. Franz turned to go. "Come back,"
The Woman called, "I'm ready now,"
But was she? And what about Franz? He didn't dare
Return. An hour later, the woman
In a faded robe sat in the kitchen, playing
Solitaire, and Franz lay down
Beside the corpse and slept, unloved, untouched
In the chill, moon-flooded garden air.

Ruins

Not far from the palace
the air was filled with haze
that swept, unhindered, into every open place,
and the sea like a blue quilt
swelled and came apart.
Its blistered scrolls of stuffing littered the shore.
The King was pleased. 'Great passions
seek release,' he thought.
Up the road, over the tawny seaside barrens
the sound of a flute caught his ear.
An old hotel, surrounded by arcades
and flanked by towers, lay just ahead.
The water in the swimming pool was clear
and marble gods and goddesses stood around.
Beyond an avenue of trees, half-open books
were scattered on the lawn for visitors who liked to read.
The King spread out his arms and cried,
'I'd love to stay, but can't.'
Farther on, packs of dogs waded in the waves
of rising heat or drowsed in the momentary shade
of a passing cloud. Trees, sagging with leaves,
hemmed in small tracts of all-white bungalows.
Shafts of heavy sunlight struck the ground.
Beside a house, next to a wood, a woman
in a bathing suit was hanging up her wash.
The King took off his crown and went to her.
Later, rising from the bed, he thought,
'Have all my royal moments come to this?'
He patted her behind and motored off.
Two men were fishing from a boat, two others
watching from the shore. The stillness
of the scene filled him with remorse.
Was it craving for the unknown

that drove him over the dappled countryside?
If a genius finds his subjects far from his life,
why shouldn't a king? He parked the car.
In the lilac-scented air, under the fuss of starlight,
the dusty sickle of the moon, he stood alone.
The fields unfolding from his feet
were coated with the ashes of decease.
He waited for the buried bird to sing,
for the dark mother to rise close by.
He listened for the wordless tirades of the wind.
He closed his eyes. There was nothing
in the ruins of the night that was not his.

RICHARD TILLINGHAST

Savannah, Sleepless

A bell has rung twelve times.
Once.
Twice.
Could I be the last non-sleeper abroad in Savannah?
Elevators have been upgathered
and then, with me in one, sent down again.

To the hotel lounge.
Duels and steam locomotives
hang on its baize walls.
Billiard balls stand expectantly,
in their round way.

Two people begin to become musical.
Powder-puff, honey-dark skin, pink gown with springy straps:
she can kiss a passing cheek and keep singing.
He tickles the ivories
and smiles with his voice, like Nat "King" Cole.
A machine plays the beat for their song.

Two men discuss two women.
Chairs are drawn up.
Names are given.
A notebook sits apart,
entranced by the yin-yang of brandy and cigar.

No, evidently, I am not the last waking human
in the Hilton Hotel.
The singer is explaining she doesn't want

to set the world on fire,
she just wants to start a flame in the heart
of some unspecified "you."

Outside, the million tongues of the city sleep,
and the Atlantic draws a breath.

Firstness

Early pleasures please best, some old voice whispers:
Cozy holdings, the heart's iambic thud
And sly wanderings—lip-touchings, long summers,
The rain's pourings and pipings heard from bed,
Earth-smell of old houses, airy ceilings,
A boy's brainy and indolent imaginings.

Twenty summers gone then that boy is gone,
Speeding down beach roads in a friend's MG.
Love, or the limey buzz of a g & t—
Or better, both—and the watery hunter's moon,
Accelerate the engines of the night,
And set a long chase afoot.

Today, twenty years older than that even,
I breathe quietness and fresh-laundered linen,
Kneeling, seeing with eyes opened white brick,
Smelling Sunday, mumbling beside my son those words
About a lost sheep, and someone's having erred.
Thank God for instinct, and beginner's luck.

ELLEN BRYANT VOIGT

Landscape, Dense with Trees

When you move away, you see how much depends
on the pace of the days, how much
depended on the haze we waded through
each summer—visible heat, wavy and discursive
as the lazy track of the snake in the dusty road;
and on the habit in town of porches thatched in vines,
and in the country long dense promenades, the way
we sacrificed the yards to shade.
It was partly the heat that made my father
plant so many trees: two maples marking the site
for the house, two elms on either side when it was done;
mimosa by the fence, and as it failed, fast-growing chestnuts,
loblolly pines; and dogwood, redbud, ornamental crab.
On the farm, everything else he grew
something could eat, but this
would be a permanent mark of his industry,
a glade established in the open field. Or so it seemed.
Looking back at the empty house from across the hill,
I see how well the house is camouflaged, see how
that porous fence of saplings, their later
scrim of foliage, thickened around it,
and he still had chinked and mortared, planting more.
Last August, although he'd lost all tolerance for heat,
he backed the truck in at the family grave
and stood in the truckbed all afternoon, pruning
the landmark oak, repairing recent damage by a wind;
then he came home and hung a swing in one
of the horse chestnuts for my visit.
The heat was a hand at his throat,
a fist to his weak heart. But it made a triumph

of the cooler air inside, in the bedroom,
in the maple bedstead where he slept,
in the brick house nearly swamped by leaves.

The Lotus Flowers

The surface of the pond was mostly green—
bright green algae reaching out from the banks,
then the mass of water lilies, their broad round leaves
rim to rim, each white flower spreading
from the center of a green saucer.
We teased and argued, choosing the largest,
the sweetest bloom, but when the rowboat
lumbered through and rearranged them,
we found the plants were anchored, the separate
muscular stems descending in the dense water—
only the most determined put her hand
into that frog-slimed pond
to wrestle with a flower. Back and forth
we pumped across the water, in twos and threes,
full of brave adventure. On the marshy shore,
the others hollered for their turns,
or at the hem of where we pitched the tents
gathered firewood—

                this was wilderness,
although the pond was less than half an acre
and we could still see the grand magnolias
in the village cemetery, their waxy
white conical blossoms gleaming in the foliage.
A dozen girls, the oldest only twelve, two sisters
with their long braids, my shy neighbor,
someone squealing without interruption—
all we didn't know about the world buoyed us

as the frightful water sustained and moved the flowers
tethered at a depth we couldn't see.

In the late afternoon, before they'd folded
into candles on the dark water,
I went to fill the bucket at the spring.
Deep in the pines, exposed tree roots
formed a natural arch, a cave of black loam.
I raked off the skin of leaves and needles,
leaving a pool so clear and shallow
I could count the pebbles
on the studded floor. The sudden cold
splashing up from the bucket to my hands
made me want to plunge my hand in—
and I held it under, feeling the shock that wakes
and deadens, watching first my fingers,
then the ledge beyond me,
the snake submerged and motionless,
the head propped on its coils the way a girl
crosses her arms before her on the sill
and rests her chin there.

Lugging the bucket back to the noisy clearing,
I found nothing changed, the boat
still rocked across the pond,
the fire straggled and cracked as we fed it
branches and debris into the night,
leaning back on our pallets—
spokes in a wheel—learning the names of the many
constellations, learning how each fixed
cluster took its name:
not from the strongest light but from the pattern
made by stars of lesser magnitude,
so like the smaller stars we rowed among.

The Storm

After trimming the split trunk of our tallest maple,
we drove along the littered road to see
the other damage. On the next high ground,
the neighbors' white frame house was still intact
but their porch was lined in black—like silk, that soft
when we touched it—a jagged hole where the switch box
used to be, where lightning entered. Indoors,
it had traced a map on the walls
as it traveled the wires behind the walls,
throwing out at every socket fists of fire only inches
from where they sat. No one had been hurt, no one
shocked or burned, but each needed
to tell us what had happened, still figuring
whether to count their luck as bad or good.

We took the long way back to check the creek
loosened from its channel into the fields,
crowding the cattle to an upper ridge,
the young sycamores along the bank
shorter now by half, forking
at water level, and the water red as rust,
swift, swirling the whipped limbs of the willow-oaks,
grazing the concrete bridge and full of trash.
My father explained the bloated lumps
as logs, or broken fence, and pointed out
the occasional shimmering arrow at the surface—
something alive and swimming with the current—

trying to make it all seem natural,
as my mother had calmed us
in the noise and flash and passion
we'd shuddered through the night before.
But already a smell was rising from the new river,

the bottomland, the small lost animals it swallowed.
And we were learning risk and consequence,
having seen the neighbors' yard:
strips of rubber in the trees and grass,
the poles unattached, the central silver cord
simply missing, that carried power in.

Short Story

My grandfather killed a mule with a hammer,
or maybe with a plank, or a stick, maybe
it was a horse—the story varied
in the telling. If he was planting corn
when it happened, it was a mule, and he was plowing
the upper slope, west of the house, his overalls
stiff to the knees with red dirt, the lines
draped behind his neck.
He must have been glad to rest
when the mule first stopped mid-furrow;
looked back at where he'd come, then down
to the brush along the creek he meant to clear.
No doubt he noticed the hawk's great leisure
over the field, the crows lumped
in the biggest elm on the opposite hill.
After he'd wiped his hatbrim with his sleeve,
he called to the mule as he slapped the line
along its rump, clicked and whistled.

My grandfather was a slight, quiet man,
smaller than most women, smaller
than his wife. Had she been in the yard,
seen him heading toward the pump now,
she'd pump for him a dipper of cold water.
Walking back to the field, past the corncrib,

he took an ear of corn to start the mule,
but the mule was planted. He never cursed
or shouted, only whipped it, the mule
rippling its backside each time
the switch fell, and when that didn't work
whipped it low on its side, where it's tender,
then cross-hatched the welts he'd made already.
The mule went down on one knee,
and that was when he reached for the blown limb,
or walked to the pile of seasoning lumber; or else,
unhooked the plow and took his own time to the shed
to get the hammer.   By the time I was born,
he couldn't even lift a stick. He lived
another fifteen years in a chair,
but now he's dead, and so is his son,
who never meant to speak a word against him,
and whom I never asked what his father
was planting and in which field,
and whether it happened before he married,
before his children came in quick succession,
before his wife died of the last one.
And only a few of us are left
who ever heard that story.

The Farmer

In the still-blistering late afternoon,
like currying a horse the rake
circled the meadow, the cut grass ridging
behind it. This summer, if the weather held,
he'd risk a second harvest after years
of reinvesting, leaving fallow.
These fields were why he farmed—

he walked the fenceline like a man in love.
The animals were merely what he needed: cattle
and pigs; chickens for a while; a drayhorse,
saddle horses he was paid to pasture—
an endless stupid round
of animals, one of them always hungry, sick, lost,
calving or farrowing, or waiting slaughter.

When the field began dissolving in the dusk,
he carried feed down to the knoll,
its clump of pines, gate, trough, lick, chute
and two gray hives; leaned into the Jersey's side
as the galvanized bucket filled with milk;
released the cow and turned to the bees.
He'd taken honey before without protection.
This time, they could smell something
in his sweat—fatigue? impatience,
although he was a stubborn, patient man?
Suddenly, like flame, they were swarming over him.
He rolled in the dirt, manure and stiff hoof-prints,
started back up the path, rolled in the fresh hay—
refused to run, which would have pumped
the venom through him faster—passed the oaks
at the yard's edge, rolled in the yard, reached
the kitchen, and when he tore off his clothes
crushed bees dropped from him like scabs.

For a week he lay in the darkened bedroom.
The doctor stopped by twice a day—
the hundred stings "enough to kill an ox,
enough to kill a younger man." What saved him
were the years of smaller doses—
like minor disappointments,
instructive poison, something he could use.

DAVID WAGONER

On Motel Walls

Beyond the foot of the bed: a seascape whose ocean,
Under the pummelling of a moon the shape and shade
Of a wrecking ball, is breaking into slabs
Against a concrete coast. Next to the closet:
A landscape of pasty mountains no one could climb
Or fall from, beyond whose sugary grandeur
Lies Flatland, a blankness plastered on plasterboard.
And over the bed: a garden in the glare
Of shadowless noon where flowerheads burst more briefly
And emptily and finally than fireworks.

For hours, I've been a castaway on that shore
By that fake water where nothing was ever born,
Where the goddess of beauty sank. I've flopped on those slopes
Where no one on earth could catch a breath worth breathing,
And I've been caught in that garden
Where the light is neither waves nor particles
But an inorganic splatter without a source.

Tonight, what's in the eye of this beholder
Is less and less and all the ways I can go
Wrong myself through the quick passing
Of sentences: tomorrow, I may be staring
Straight in the face of the hanging judge of my future
Who'll read me with the deadpan of a jailer
Before a search, a lock-down, and lights out.
I'll do hard time all night inside these walls
In my mind's eye, a transient facing a door
That says, *Have you forgotten anything*
Of value? Have you left anything behind?

Photographing a Rattlesnake

On smooth sand among stones
It stares more steadily
And lidlessly than the lens
Held near it, not hiding
Or posing, but simply there
In a dead calm, dead sure
Of the ways of its body
Around the maze past the end
Of nerves to the inmost
Rattle, but suddenly
The wedge of the blunt
Straightforward head, S-curve
Of muscle straight
Forward in a blur, mouth wide
For a down-slanted stabbing
Of fangs, a thump
At the camera's glassy eye,
Then a slow turning-away
Out of spirals from the sun
To shadows, to be scattered
Out of plain sight
Into mica spilled on pebbles
Over diamonds seen through
A teardrop of venom
Back to its still life.

By a Waterfall

Over the sheer stone cliff-face, over springs and star clusters
Of maidenhair giving in and in to the spray
Through thorn-clawed crookshanks

And gnarled root-ends like vines where the sun has never from dawn
To noon or dusk come spilling its cascades,
The stream is falling, at the brink
Blue-green but whitening and changing to pale rain
And falling farther, not as rain or as mist
But both now, water
Doing what it must, exchanging all for all over all
Around and past our shapes to a dark-green pool
Below, where it tumbles
Over another verge to become a stream once more
Downstream in curving slopes through a headlong
Cloud of what it was
And will be, and beside it, we share the storm of its arrival,
Its constant transformations into a source,
A fulfillment, a leavetaking.

Sharp-shin

He broke past the corners
Of our eyes before we could see, before
We could quite catch
Sight of him already beyond
The fence and the next yard and back
Again in full flight, the sharp-shinned
Hawk, an amber and slate streak
Through the morning air after
A blur of a pine siskin, zigzagging
But (like our eyes) not quite touching it, not quite
Taking it in a swirling S-curve
Through vine maple up in a flare
Of tail stripes and dark coverts
To a hemlock branch to perch
Dead still, his claws empty.

Still breathing, we waited. The towhees,
The song sparrows, the juncoes
Huddled in thickets, and the quick yellow-
And-gray-streaked siskins flocked
Quivering in a firtree,
Waiting. The whole broad yard
Fell silent, and nothing moved
Anywhere, not even the one cloud.

He waited too, his breast the shade
Of dead leaves, his blue-gray wings
Folded like bark. The dimmed firecoals
Of his eyes held all of us
There, slow minute
After minute, where we were.

Finally, gradually, one siskin forgot
Where it was, where it had been and why
It had ever been afraid, remembered
Simply wanting to be
Somewhere else that moment and flew
At last from there only
To there in the open, and instantly
So swiftly nothing could know
Exactly when he began the sharp-shin
Burst out of cover around
And up in a tight swerve, struck
Without a pause, and was gone
Deep through the green tree-crown
That made no stir or murmur,
And all fell still once more
While out of his sharp talons
The sharper hook of his beak
Took its share of spring.

ROBERT PENN WARREN

Far West Once

Aloud, I said, with a slight stir of heart,
"The last time"—and thought, years thence, to a time
When only in memory I might
Repeat this last tramp up the shadowy gorge
In the mountains, cabinward, the fall
Coming on, the aspen leaf gold, sun low
At the western end of the gun-barrel passage
Waiting, waiting the trigger-touch
And the blast of darkness, the target me.

I said, "I'll try to remember as much
As a man caught in Time cannot forget,"
For I carried a headful of summer, and knew
That I'd never again, in the gloaming, walk
Up that trail, now lulled by the stone-song of waters;
Nor again on path pebbles, noon-plain, see
The old rattler's fat belly twist and distend
As it coiled, and the rattles up from dust rise
To vibrate mica-bright, in the sun's beam;
Nor again, from below, on the cliff's over-thrust,
Catch a glimpse of the night-crouching cougar's eyes
That, in my flashlight's strong beam, had burned
Coal-bright as they swung,
Detached, contemptuous, and slow,
Into the pine woods' mounting mass
Of darkness that, eventually,
Ahead, would blot out, star by star,
The slot of the sky-slice that now I
Moved under, and on to dinner and bed.

And to sleep—and even in sleep to feel
The nag and pretensions of day dissolve
And flow away in that musical murmur
Of waters; then to wake in dark with some strange
Heart-hope, undefinable, verging to tears
Of happiness and the soul's calm.

How long ago! But in years since,
On other trails, in the shadow of
What other cliffs, in lands whose names
Crank on the tongue, I have felt my boots
Crush gravel, or press the soundlessness
Of detritus of pine or fir, and heard
Movement of water, far, how far—

Or waking under nameless stars,
Have heard such redemptive music, from
Distance to distance threading starlight,
Able yet, as long ago,
Despite scum of wastage and scab of years,
To touch again the heart, as though at a dawn
Of dew-bright Edenic promise, with,
Far off, far off, in verdurous shade, first birdsong.

Youthful Picnic Long Ago: Sad Ballad on Box

In Tennessee once the campfire glowed
With steady joy in its semi-globe
Defined by the high-arched nave of oaks against
Light-years of stars and the
Last soundless scream space makes beyond space. Faces,

In grave bemusement, leaned, eyes fixed
On the fingers white in their delicate dance
On the strings of the box. And delicate
Was the melancholy that swelled each heart, and timed
The pulse in wrist, and wrist, and wrist—all while
The face leaned over the box
In shadow of hair that in fire-light down-gleamed,
Smoother than varnish, and black. And like
A silver vine that upward to darkness twines,
The voice confirmed the sweet sadness
Young hearts gave us no right to.

No right to, yet. Though some day would,
As Time unveiled,
In its own dancing parody of grace,
The bony essence of each joke on joke.

But even back then perhaps we knew
That the dancing fingers enacted
A truth far past the pain declared
By that voice that somehow made pain sweet.

Would it be better or worse, if now
I could name the names I've lost, and see,
Virile or beautiful, those who, entranced, leaned.
I wish I knew what wisdom they had there learned.

The singer—her name, it flees the fastest!
If only she'd toss back that varnished black screen
Of beautiful hair, and let
Flame reveal the grave cheek-curve, eye-shine,
Then I'd know that much.
If not her name.

Even now.

Why You Climbed Up

Where, vomit-yellow, the lichen crawls
Up the boulder, where the rusty needle
Falls from the pine to pad earth's silence
Against what intrusive foot may come, you come—
But come not knowing where or why.
Like substance hangs the silence of
The afternoon. Look—you will see
The tiny glint of the warbler's eye, see
The beak, half-open, in still heat gasp, see
Moss on a cliff, where water oozes.

Where or why,
You wonder, wandering, with sweat and pant,
Up the mountain's heave and clamber,
As though to forget and leave
All things, great and small, you call
The past, all things, great and small, you call
The Self, and remember only how once
In the moonlit Pacific you swam west, hypnotized
By stroke on stroke, the rhythm that
Filled all the hollow head and was
The only self you carried with you then.

What brought you back?
You can't remember now,
And do not guess that years from now you may not remember
How once, on this high ridge, seeing
The sun blaze down on the next and higher horizon,
You turned, and bumbled for some old logging road
To follow, stumbling, down.

Then all begins again. And you are you.

Old-Time Childhood in Kentucky

When I was a boy I saw the world I was in.
I saw it for what it was. Canebrakes with
Track beaten down by bear paw. Tobacco,
In endless rows, the pink inner flesh of black fingers
Crushing to green juice tobacco worms plucked
From a leaf. The great trout,
Motionless, poised in the shadow of his
Enormous creek-boulder.
But the past and the future broke on me, as I got older.

Strange, into the past I first grew. I handled the old bullet-mold.
I drew out a saber, touched an old bayonet, I dreamed
Of the death-scream. Old spurs I tried on.
The first great General Jackson had ridden just north to our state
To make a duel legal—or avoid the law.
It was all for honor. He said: "I would have killed him
Even with his hot lead in my heart." This for honor. I longed
To understand. I said the magic word.
I longed to say it aloud, to be heard.

I saw the strategy of Bryce's Crossroads, saw
The disposition of troops at Austerlitz, but knew
It was far away, long ago. I saw
The marks of the old man's stick in the dust, heard
The old voice explaining. His eyes weren't too good,
So I read him books he wanted. Read him
Breasted's *History of Egypt*. Saw years uncoil like a snake.
I built a pyramid with great care. There interred
Pharoah's splendor and might.
Excavation next summer exposed that glory to man's sight.

At a cave mouth my uncle showed me crinoid stems,
And in limestone skeletons of the fishy form of some creature.
"All once under water," he said, "no saying the millions

Of years." He walked off, the old man still with me. "Grandpa,"
I said, "What do you do, things being like this?" "All you can,"
He said, looking off through treetops, skyward. "Love
Your wife, love your get, keep your word, and
If need arises die for what men die for. There aren't
Many choices.
And remember that truth doesn't always live in the number of voices."

He hobbled away. The woods seemed darker. I stood
In the encroachment of shadow. I shut
My eyes, head thrown back, eyelids black.
I stretched out the arm on each side, and, waterlike,
Wavered from knees and hips, feet yet firm-fixed, it seemed
On shells, in mud, in sand, in stone, as though
In eons back I grew there in that submarine
Depth and lightlessness, waiting to discover
What I would be, might be, after ages—how many?—had rolled over.

True Love

In silence the heart raves. It utters words
Meaningless, that never had
A meaning. I was ten, skinny, red-headed,

Freckled. In a big black Buick,
Driven by a big grown boy, with a necktie, she sat
In front of the drugstore, sipping something

Through a straw. There is nothing like
Beauty. It stops your heart. It
Thickens your blood. It stops your breath. It

Makes you feel dirty. You need a hot bath.
I leaned against a telephone pole, and watched.
I thought I would die if she saw me.

How could I exist in the same world with that brightness?
Two years later she smiled at me. She
Named my name. I thought I would wake up dead.

Her grown brothers walked with the bent-knee
Swagger of horsemen. They were slick-faced.
Told jokes in the barbershop. Did no work.

Their father was what is called a drunkard.
Whatever he was he stayed on the third floor
Of the big white farmhouse under the maples for twenty-five years.

He never came down. They brought everything up to him.
I did not know what a mortgage was.
His wife was a good, Christian woman, and prayed.

When the daughter got married, the old man came down wearing
An old tail coat, the pleated shirt yellowing.
The sons propped him. I saw the wedding. There were

Engraved invitations, it was so fashionable. I thought
I would cry. I lay in bed that night
And wondered if she would cry when something was done to her.

The mortgage was foreclosed. That word was whispered.
She never came back. The family
Sort of drifted off. Nobody wears shiny boots like that now.

But I know she is beautiful forever, and lives
In a beautiful house, far away.
She called my name once. I didn't even know she knew it.

JAMES WHITEHEAD

A Natural Theology

Once again a spring has come around
And many of the best I think I know
Are going crazy.
                Light on the warm ground
Is almost God requiring them to grow—
Or, at least, to change—the usual song
And arrogant demand that nature makes
Of moral, thoughtful people all gone wrong
So far as they can see.
                      Their hands hold rakes.
They comb what later are attractive lawns.
They harrow in their ways, then drive the stakes
Up which flowers and food will climb their dream
Of this one season right.
                    They pick up sticks
To make the whole thing work, then plant a tree.
Spring. Spring. They take it personally.

How It Seemed to Him Away from Home

I'm out of town and visiting old friends,
Old girls and boys of the successful worlds,
And the talk is serious, pretty good
Especially about the things amends
Should be made for: not answering the mail,
Lying through your teeth when the God damned lie
Is obvious, going for the new wife
Of your running buddy, or the husband. Whatever.—

And then some talk about our friends who've died,
Going over names, going for their throats
Long out of sight, drinking and going on
To arguing about the minds of cats.—
"Do birds at dawn *intend* to greet the sun?"

—Pretty damned strong to face, after the dead,
The minds of beasts, and then our mad

Who though not legion are not few,
Who are not dead, are satisfied in small rooms
Or wandering around on barbered lawns
Not far away, or dully gone to bed
With only now and then some troubled dreams.—

"We're close to them, if they're on earth,
Breath by breath,"
Somebody said poetically in bad faith.

For Ellen after the Publication
of Her Stories

You do sunrise as well as anyone
But the dark phone ringing before false dawn
And hours before the actual grey light
Is a mean surprise and no astonishment.—
Hearing it clatter in your dream you fight
As usual to recollect the plot
And know the theme escapes you. You're awake

And you are listening to someone drink
And she is not about your family—
Your sons, parents, brothers, grandchildren
Or any friend or lover at your heart.
She is a lady who will praise your book.
She says she knows you've lived outrageously.
How can you write about such things as happen?
She knows about the night
Of the wildest story, for she was there.
She wasn't. She's nearly crazy with The Fear.
She says no man is fair.
By now you are remembering her life,
While listening to the soft extraordinary sounds of grief.

RICHARD WILBUR

Lying

To claim, at a dead party, to have spotted a grackle,
When in fact you haven't of late, can do no harm.
Your reputation for saying things of interest
Will not be marred, if you hasten to other topics,
Nor will the delicate web of human trust
Be ruptured by that airy fabrication.
Later, however, talking with toxic zest
Of golf, or taxes, or the rest of it
Where the beaked ladle plies the chuckling ice,
You may enjoy a chill of severance, hearing
Above your head the shrug of unreal wings.
Not that the world is tiresome in itself:
We know what boredom is: it is a dull
Impatience or a fierce velleity,
A champing wish, stalled by our lassitude,
To make or do. In the strict sense, of course,
We invent nothing, merely bearing witness
To what each morning brings again to light:
Gold crosses, cornices, astonishment
Of panes, the turbine-vent which natural law
Spins on the grill-end of the diner's roof,
Then grass and grackles or, at the end of town
In sheen-swept pastureland, the horse's neck
Clothed with its usual thunder, and the stones
Beginning now to tug their shadows in
And track the air with glitter. All these things
Are there before us; there before we look
Or fail to look; there to be seen or not
By us, as by the bee's twelve thousand eyes,

According to our means and purposes.
So too with strangeness not to be ignored,
Total eclipse or snow upon the rose,
And so with that most rare conception, nothing.
What is it, after all, but something missed?
It is the water of a dried-up well
Gone to assail the cliffs of Labrador.
There is what galled the arch-negator, sprung
From Hell to probe with intellectual sight
The cells and heavens of a given world
Which he could take but as another prison:
Small wonder that, pretending not to be,
He drifted through the bar-like boles of Eden
In a *black mist low creeping*, dragging down
And darkening with moody self-absorption
What, when he left it, lifted and, if seen
From the sun's vantage, seethed with vaulting hues.
Closer to making than the deftest fraud
Is seeing how the catbird's tail was made
To counterpoise, on the mock-orange spray,
Its light, up-tilted spine; or, lighter still,
How the shucked tunic of an onion, brushed
To one side on a backlit chopping-board
And rocked by trifling currents, prints and prints
Its bright, ribbed shadow like a flapping sail.
Odd that a thing is most itself when likened:
The eye mists over, basil hints of clove,
The river glazes toward the dam and spills
To the drubbed rocks below its crashing cullet,
And in the barnyard near the sawdust-pile
Some great thing is tormented. Either it is
A tarp torn loose and in the groaning wind
Now puffed, now flattened, or a hip-shot beast
Which tries again, and once again, to rise.
What, though for pain there is no other word,

Finds pleasure in the cruellest simile?
It is something in us like the catbird's song
From neighbor bushes in the grey of morning
That, harsh or sweet, and of its own accord,
Proclaims its many kin. It is a chant
Of the first springs, and it is tributary
To the great lies told with the eyes half-shut
That have the truth in view: the tale of Chiron
Who, with sage head, wild heart, and planted hoof
Instructed brute Achilles in the lyre,
Or of the garden where we first mislaid
Simplicity of wish and will, forgetting
Out of what cognate splendor all things came
To take their scattering names; and nonetheless
That matter of a baggage-train surprised
By a few Gascons in the Pyrenees
Which, having worked three centuries and more
In the dark caves of France, poured out at last
The blood of Roland, who to Charles his king
And to the dove that hatched the dove-tailed world
Was faithful unto death, and shamed the Devil.

Hamlen Brook

    At the alder-darkened brink
  Where the stream slows to a lucid jet
I lean to the water, dinting its top with sweat,
    And see, before I can drink,

    A startled inchling trout
  Of spotted near-transparency,
Trawling a shadow solider than he.
    He swerves now, darting out

To where, in a flicked slew
Of sparks and glittering silt, he weaves
Through stream-bed rocks, disturbing foundered leaves,
And butts then out of view

Beneath a sliding glass
Crazed by the skimming of a brace
Of burnished dragon-flies across its face,
In which deep cloudlets pass

And a white precipice
Of mirrored birch-trees plunges down
Toward where the azures of the zenith drown.
How shall I drink all this?

Joy's trick is to supply
Dry lips with what can cool and slake,
Leaving them dumbstruck also with an ache
Nothing can satisfy.

The Ride

The horse beneath me seemed
To know what course to steer
Through the horror of snow I dreamed,
And so I had no fear,

Nor was I chilled to death
By the wind's white shudders, thanks
To the veils of his patient breath
And the mist of sweat from his flanks.

It seemed that all night through,
Within my hand no rein
And nothing in my view
But the pillar of his mane,

I rode with magic ease
At a quick, unstumbling trot
Through shattering vacancies
On into what was not,

Till the weave of the storm grew thin,
With a threading of cedar-smoke,
And the ice-blind pane of an inn
Shimmered, and I awoke.

How shall I now get back
To the inn-yard where he stands,
Burdened with every lack,
And waken the stable-hands

To give him, before I think
That there was no horse at all,
Some hay, some water to drink,
A blanket and a stall?

The Catch

From the dress-box's plashing tis-
Sue paper she pulls out her prize,
Dangling it to one side before my eyes
Like a weird sort of fish

That she has somehow hooked and gaffed
And on the dock-end holds in air—
Limp, corrugated, lank, a catch too rare
Not to be photographed.

I, in my chair, make shift to say
Some bright, discerning thing, and fail,
Proving once more the blindness of the male.
Annoyed, she stalks away

And then is back in half a minute,
Consulting, now, not me at all
But the long mirror, mirror on the wall.
The dress, now that she's in it,

Has changed appreciably, and gains
By lacy shoes, a light perfume
Whose subtle field electrifies the room,
And two slim golden chains.

With a fierce frown and hard-pursed lips
She twists a little on her stem
To test the even swirling of the hem,
Smooths down the waist and hips,

Plucks at the shoulder-straps a bit,
Then turns around and looks behind,
Her face transfigured now by peace of mind.
There is no question—it

Is wholly charming, it is she,
As I belatedly remark,
And may be hung now in the fragrant dark
Of her soft armory.

Orchard Trees, January

It's not the case, though some might wish it so
Who from a window watch the blizzard blow

White riot through their branches vague and stark,
That they keep snug beneath their pelted bark.

They take affliction in until it jells
To crystal ice between their frozen cells,

And each of them is inwardly a vault
Of jewels rigorous and free of fault,

Unglimpsed by us until in May it bears
A sudden crop of green-pronged solitaires.

NANCY WILLARD

Lullaby for Familiars

Lullaby, my little cat,
Lord of Mouse and Knave of Bat
Hail, Mischief, full of grace,
who did lately love this place.

Lullaby your crescent claws
in the chambers of your paws
which you sharpen day and night,
keeping all my kettles bright.

Lullaby your gentle purr.
What sad spirits did you lure
to the mushroom rings I made
and the lesser spells we laid?

Lullaby your pebbled tongue.
Keep my velvets ever young.
Keep my broomsticks ever slick
with the patience of a lick.

Lullaby your lively tail.
Never have I see it fail,
devils gone and revels done,
to point the quickest highway home.

Eternal life, eternal death
hang on our Creator's breath.
Little tiger in God's eye,
remember Nancy's lullaby.

Science Fiction

Here, said the spirit,
is the Diamond Planet.
Shall I change you into a diamond?
No? Then let us proceeed
to the Red Planet,
desert star,
rocks too young to know
lichens. There's plenty
of room. Stay as long
as you like. You don't like?
Then let us go forth to
the Planet of Mists,
the veiled bride,
the pleasures of losing and finding,
the refinement of symbols.
She's all yours.

I see you looking at that blue planet.
It's mostly water.
The land's crowded with
creatures. You have mists
but they rain, diamonds
but they cost. You have
only one moon.
You have camels and babies and cigars
but everything grows up
or wears out.
And on clear nights
you have the stars
without having them.

A Wreath to the Fish

Who is this fish, still wearing its wealth,
flat on my drainboard, dead asleep
its suit of mail proof only against the stream?
What is it to live in a stream,
to dwell forever in a tunnel of cold,
never to leave your shining birthsuit,
never to spend your inheritance of thin coins?
And who is the stream, who lolls all day
in an unmade bed, living on nothing but weather,
singing, a little mad in the head,
opening her apron to shells, carcasses, crabs,
eyeglasses, the lines of fishermen begging for
news from the interior—oh, who are these lines
that link a big sky to a small stream
that go down for great things:
the cold muscle of the trout,
the shining scrawl of the eel in a difficult passage,
hooked—but who is this hook, this cunning
and faithful fanatic who will not let go
but holds the false bait and the true worm alike
and tears the fish, yet gives it up to the basket
in which it will ride to the kitchen
of someone important, perhaps the Pope
who rejoices that his cook has found such a fish
and blesses it and eats it and rises, saying,
"Children, what is it to live in the stream,
day after day, and come at last to the table,
transfigured with spices and herbs
a little martyr, a little miracle;
children, children, who is this fish?"

⋆ *Wreath: a poem in the shape of a circle, that ends where it began.*

Poem Made of Water

Praise to my text, Water, which taught me writing,
and praise to the five keepers of the text,
water in Ocean, water in River, water in Lake,
water in cupped hands, water in Tears. Praise
for River, who says: Travel to the source,
poling your raft of words, mindful of currents,
avoiding confusion, delighting in danger
when its spines sparkle, yet keeping
your craft upright, your sentence alive.
You have been sentenced to life.

Praise for Ocean and her generous lesson,
that a great poem changes from generation to generation,
that any reader may find his treasure there
and even the landlocked heart wants to travel.
Praise for that heart, for its tides,
for tiny pools winking in rocks
like poems which make much of small matters:
five snails, two limpets, a closely watched
minnow, his spine a zipper,
and a white stone wearing the handprints of dead coral.

Praise for Tears, which are faithful to grief
not by urns but by understatement.
Praise for thirst, for order in the eye and in the ear
and in the heart, and for water in cupped hands,
for the poem that slakes thirst
and the poem that wakes it.
Praise for Lake, which bustles with swimmers at noon.
I have been one, busy under the light,
piling rocks into castles, not seeing
my work under the ruffled water.

And later—the lake still sleepy in the last light—
the castle squats like the rough draft of a prayer,
disguised as a castle, which tells me
to peer into the dark and interpret shapes in the ooze:
the row boat rising like a beak, the oil drum rusting,
the pop bottles fisted in weeds, every sunken
thing still, without purpose, dreamed over
till the fisherman's net brings up—
what? a bronze mask? a torso of softest marble?

Go deep. Save, sift, pack, lose, find again.
Come back as snow, rain, tears, crest and foam.
Come back to baptize, heal, drown.
Come back as Water. Come back as Poem.

MILLER WILLIAMS

A Poem for Emily

Small fact and fingers and farthest one from me,
a hand's width and two generations away,
in this still present I am fifty three.
You are not yet a full day.

When I am sixty three, when you are ten,
and you are neither closer nor as far,
your arms will fill with what you know by then,
the arithmetic and love we do and are.

When I by blood and luck am eighty six
and you are some place else and thirty three
believing in sex and god and politics
with children who look not at all like me,

some time I know you will have read them this
so they will know I love them and say so
and love their mother. Child, whatever is
is always or never was. Long ago,

a day I watched a while beside your bed,
I wrote this down, a thing that might be kept
a while, to tell you what I would have said
when you were who knows what and I was dead
which is I stood and loved you while you slept.

After the Revolution for Jesus
the Associate Professor Prepares His Final Remarks

What the blind lost when radio
gave way to TV,
what the deaf lost when movies
stopped spelling out words and spoke,
was a way back in. Always, this desire
to be inside again, when the doors are closed.

On the other side of the doors
our friends and parents and grandparents
work and eat and read books and make sense and love.

The thought of being disconnected
from history or place can empty the heart;
we are most afraid,
whatever else we fear,
of feeling the memory go, and of exile.
And death, which is both at once.

Still, as our lives
are the inhalations and exhalations of gods
we ought not fear those things we know will come
and ought not hope for what we know will not.
The dogs that waited for soldiers to come home
from Phillipi, New Guinea, Pennsylvania,
are all dead now whether or not the men
came back to call them.
There is no constancy but a falling away
with only love as a temporary stay
and not much assurance of that.

The desert religions are founded on sandy ways
to set ourselves free from that endless tumbling downward.
Thus we endow ourselves with gods of purpose,
the purposes of gods, and do their battles.

We are sent to war for money, but we go for god.

Prison is no place for living
but for reliving lives.
I remember a quarrel of students
proving, reproving the world;
a woman taking love
she didn't want, but needed
like a drowning swimmer
thrown a strand of barbed wire
by a kind stranger standing on the shore.

Imperfect love in that imperfect world
seemed elegant and right.
Now the old air that shaped itself to our bodies
will take the forms of others.
They will laugh with this air and pass it through their bodies
but days like ours
they will not come again to this poor planet.

I am reinventing our days together.
A man should be careful with words
at a time like this,
but lies have some attraction over the truth;
there is something in deceitful words
that sounds good to the ear.

The first layer of paint conceals the actor;
the second conceals the paint.

By which sly truth we have come to where we are.

I can hear brief choirs of rifles.
Inside my head
naked women wander toward my bed.
How gently they lie there, loving themselves to sleep.

What do we know that matters that Aeschylus did not know?

I do believe in God, the Mother and Father,
Maker of possibility, distance and dust,
who may never come to judge or quicken the dead
but does abide. We live out our lives
inside the body of God,
a heretic and breathing universe
that feeds on the falling of sparrows
and the crumbling of nations,
the rusting away of metal
and the rotting of wood.
I will be eaten by God.
There is nothing to fear.
To die, the singers believe, is to go home.
Where should I go, going home? Lord, I am here.

CHARLES WRIGHT

March Journal

—After the Rapture comes, and everyone goes away
   Quicker than cream in a cat's mouth,
                    all of them gone
In an endless slip-knot down the sky
                    and its pink tongue
Into the black hole of Somewhere Else,

What will we do, left with the empty spaces of our lives
Intact,
      the radio frequencies still unchanged,
The same houses up for sale,
Same books unread,
          all comfort gone and its comforting . . .

For us, the earth is a turbulent rest,
               a different bed
Altogether, and kinder than that—
After the first death is the second,
A little fire in the afterglow,
           somewhere to warm your hands.

—The clean, clear line, incised, unbleeding,
   Sharp and declarative as a cut
          the instant before the blood wells out . . .

—*March Blues*
   The insides were blue, the color of Power Putty,
   When Luke dissected the dogfish,
          a plastic blue

In the whey
            sharkskin infenestrated:
Its severed tailfin bobbed like a wing-nut in another pan
As he explained the dye job
                        and what connected with what,
Its pursed lips skewed and pointed straight-lined at the ceiling,
The insides so blue, so blue . . .

March gets its second wind,
                        starlings high shine in the trees
As dread puts its left foot down and then the other.
Buds hold their breaths and sit tight.
The weeping cherries
            lower their languorous necks and nibble the grass
Sprout ends that jump head first from the ground,
Magnolia drums blue weight
                        next door when the sun is right.

—Rhythm comes from the roots of the world,
                        rehearsed and expandable.

—After the ice storm a shower of crystal down from the trees
Shattering over the ground
                        like cut glass twirling its rainbows,
Sunlight in flushed layers under the clouds,
Twirling and disappearing into the clenched March grass.

—Structure is binary, intent on a resolution,
Its parts tight but the whole loose
                        and endlessly repetitious.

—And here we stand, caught
In the crucifixal noon
                        with its bled, attendant bells,

And nothing to answer back with.
Forsythia purrs in its burning shell,
Jonquils, like Dante's angels, appear from their blue shoots.

How can we think to know of another's desire for darkness,
That low coo like a dove's
                                insistent outside the heart's window?
How can we think to think this?
How can we sit here, crossing out line after line,
Such 5-finger exercises
                        up and down, learning our scales,

And say that all quartets are eschatological
Heuristically
                when the willows swim like medusas through the trees,
Their skins beginning to blister into a 1000 green welts?
How can we think to know these things,
Clouds like full suds in the sky
                                keeping away, keeping away?

—Form is finite, an undestroyable hush over all things.

Night Journal

—I think of Issa, a man of few words:
The world of dew
Is the world of dew.
And yet . . .
And yet . . .

—Three words contain
                        all that we know for sure of the next life
Or the last one: close your eyes.

Everything else is gossip,
                              false mirrors, trick windows
Flashing like Dutch glass
In the undiminishable sun.

—I write it down in visible ink,
    Black words that disappear when held up to the light—
    I write it down
                    not to remember but to forget,
    Words like thousands of pieces of shot film
                                          exposed to the sun.
    I never see anything but the ground.

—Everyone wants to tell his story.
    The Chinese say we live in the world of the 10,000 things,
    Each of the 10,000 things
                        crying out to us
    Precisely nothing,
    A silence whose tune we've come to understand,
    Words like birthmarks,
                    embolic sunsets drying behind the tongue.
    If we were as eloquent,
    If what we say could spread the good news the way that dogwood
        does,
    Its votive candles
                        phosphorous and articulate in the green haze
    Of spring, surely something would hear us.

—Even a chip of beauty
                        is beauty intractable in the mind,
    Words the color of wind
    Moving across the fields there
                            wind-addled and wind-sprung,

Abstracted as water glints,
The fields lion-colored and rope-colored,
As in a picture of Paradise,
                          the bodies languishing over the sky
Trailing their dark identities
That drift off and sieve away to the nothingness
Behind them
                moving across the fields there
As words move, slowly, trailing their dark identities.

—Our words, like blown kisses, are swallowed by ghosts
Along the way,
                their destinations bereft
In a rub of brightness unending:
How distant everything always is,
                                  and yet how close,
Music starting to rise like smoke from under the trees.

—Birds sing an atonal row
                      unsyncopated
From tree to tree,
                dew chants
Whose songs have no words
                        from tree to tree
When night puts her dark lens in,
One on this limb, two others back there.

—Words, like all things, are caught in their finitude.
They start here, they finish here
No matter how high they rise—
                              my judgment is that I know this
And never love anything hard enough
That would stamp me
                and sink me suddenly into bliss.

PAUL ZIMMER

The Great Bird of Love over the Kingdom

I want to become a great night bird
Called The Zimmer, grow intricate gears
And tendons, brace my wings on updrafts,
Roll them down with a motion
That lifts me slowly into the stars
To fly above the troubles of the kingdom.
When I soar the moon will shine past
My shoulder and slide through
The streams like a luminous fish.
I want my cry to be huge and melancholy,
The undefiled movement of my wings
To fold and unfold on rising gloom.

People will see my silhouette from
Their windows and be comforted,
Knowing that, though oppressed,
They are cherished and watched over,
Can turn to kiss their children,
Tuck them into their beds and say:
    Sleep tight.
    No harm tonight,
    In starry skies
    The Zimmer flies.

The Place

Once in your life you pass
Through a place so pure
It becomes tainted even
By your regard, a space
Of air and trees where
Dusk comes as perfect ripeness.
Here the only sounds are
Sighs of rain and snow,
Small rustling of plants
As they unwrap in sunlight.
This is where you will go
At last when coldness comes.
It is something you realize
When you first see it,
But instantly forget.
At the end of your life
You remember and dwell in
Its faultless light forever.

Blues for Old Dogs

It's summer and the dogs decline in heat.
A time again for four letter words,
Gout, tick, mite, flea and worm.
Zimmer's dogs moan and flay themselves,
Tossing heads till their ears crack.
They dribble, pump, loll their tongues.
At night old dreams return like storms
That roam the world and come each summer
To make them tremble and dash in sleep.
These days Zimmer is a sad mutt, too.
Sometimes when the moon rises
He lays down his rancid, aging body
And says, Dear friends, come let us
Sing a little groaning song together.

BIBLIOGRAPHY OF
RECENT WORK

BIBLIOGRAPHY OF
RECENT WORK

A. R. Ammons (b. 1926), *Worldly Hopes* (1982), *Lake Country Effects* (1983)

John Ashbery (b. 1927), *Shadow Train* (1981), *A Wave* (1984)

Marvin Bell (b. 1937), *Segues: A Correspondence in Poetry* (with William Stafford) (1983), *Drawn by Stones, by Earth, by Things That Have Been in the Fire* (1984)

Wendell Berry (b. 1934), *The Wheel* (1982), *Collected Poems* (1985)

Michael Blumenthal (b. 1949), *Days We Would Rather Know* (1984), *Laps* (1984)

Philip Booth (b. 1925), *Available Light* (1976), *Before Sleep* (1980)

David Bottoms (b. 1949), *Shooting Rats at the Bibb Country Dump* (1980), *In a U-Haul North of Damascus* (1983)

Hayden Carruth (b. 1921), *The Oldest Killed Lake in North America* (1985), *Mother* (1985)

Fred Chappell (b. 1936), *Midquest* (1980), *Castel Tzingal* (1984)

John Ciardi (b. 1916), *For Instance* (1979), *Selected Poems* (1984)

Alfred Corn (b. 1943), *The Various Light* (1980), *Notes from a Child of Paradise* (1985)

Carl Dennis (b. 1939), *Signs and Wonders* (1979), *The Near World* (1985)

William Dickey (b. 1928), *Six Philosophical Songs* (1983), *Jay* (1983)

Stephen Dobyns (b. 1941), *Heat Death* (1980), *The Balthus Poems* (1984)

Rita Dove (b. 1952), *Museum* (1983), *Thomas and Beulah* (1985)

Stephen Dunn (b. 1946), *Work and Love* (1981), *Not Dancing* (1984)

Richard Eberhart (b. 1904), *Florida Poems* (1981), *The Long Reach* (1984)

John Engels (b. 1931), *The Seasons of Vermont* (1983), *Weather-Fear: New and Selected Poems, 1958–1982* (1983)

Donald Finkel (b. 1929), *What Manner of Beast* (1981), *The Detachable Man* (1984)

Jorie Graham (b. 1951), *Hybrids of Fruits and Vegetables* (1981), *Erosion* (1983)

Marilyn Hacker (b. 1942), *Taking Notice* (1980), *Assumptions* (1985)

Pamela White Hadas (b. 1946), *Designing Women* (1979), *Beside Herself* (1984)

John Haines (b. 1924), *Cicada* (1977), *News from the Glacier* (1982)

Donald Hall (b. 1928), *Kicking the Leaves* (1978), *The Toy Bone* (1979)

Anthony Hecht (b. 1923), *Aesopic* (1968), *The Venetian Vespers* (1979)

Mark Jarman (b. 1952), *The Rote Walker* (1981), *Far and Away* (1985)

Erica Jong (b. 1941), *At the Edge of the Body* (1979), *Ordinary* (1983)

Donald Justice (b. 1925), *Departures* (1973), *Selected Poems* (1979)

X. J. Kennedy (b. 1929), *Hangover Mass* (1984), *Cross Ties: Selected Poems* (1985)

Galway Kinnell (b. 1927), *Mortal Acts, Mortal Words* (1980), *Selected Poems* (1982)

Maxine Kumin (b. 1925), *Our Ground Time Here Will Be Brief: New and Selected Poems* (1982), *Closing the Ring* (1984)

Stanley Kunitz (b. 1905), *The Wellfleet Whale and Companion Poems* (1983), *Next-to-Last Things* (1985)

Sydney Lea (b. 1945), *Searching the Drowned Man* (1980), *The Floating Candles* (1983)

Philip Levine (b. 1928), *Selected Poems* (1984), *Sweet Will* (1985)

Paul Mariani (b. 1940), *Crossing Cocytus* (1982), *Prime Mover* (1985)

William Matthews (b. 1942), *Flood* (1982), *A Happy Childhood* (1984)

James Merrill (b. 1926), *The Changing Light at Sandover* (1984), *Late Settings* (1985)

Judith Moffett (b. 1942), *Keeping Time* (1976), *Whinny Moor Crossing* (1984)

Frederick Morgan (b. 1922), *Northbook* (1982), *Nine Poems* (1983)

Howard Moss (b. 1922), *Rules of Sleep* (1984), *New Selected Poems* (1985)

Carol Muske (b. 1945), *Skylight* (1981), *Windmere* (1985)

Leonard Nathan (b. 1924), *Dear Blood* (1980), *Holding Patterns* (1982)

John Frederick Nims (b. 1923), *Selected Poems* (1982), *The Kiss: A Jambalaya* (1982)

Sharon Olds (b. 1942), *Satan Says* (1980), *The Dead and the Living* (1984)

Carole Oles (b. 1939), *Quarry* (1983), *Night Watches: Inventions on the Life of Maria Mitchell* (1985)

Steven Orlen (b. 1942), *Sleeping on Doors* (1975), *Separate Creatures* (1976)

Gregory Orr (b. 1947), *Burning the Empty Nests* (1973), *The Red House* (1980)

Robert Pack (b. 1929), *Waking to My Name: New and Selected Poems* (1980), *Faces in a Single Tree* (1984)

Jay Parini (b. 1948), *Singing in Time* (1972), *Anthracite Country* (1982)

Linda Pastan (b. 1932), *PM/AM: New and Selected Poems* (1982), *A Fraction of Darkness* (1985)

Robert Pinsky (b. 1940), *An Explanation of America* (1979), *History of My Heart* (1984)

Stanley Plumly (b. 1939), *Out-of-the-Body Travel* (1979), *Summer Celestial* (1983)

Lawrence Raab (b. 1946), *Mysteries of the Horizon* (1972), *The Collector of Cold Weather* (1976)

Ira Sadoff (b. 1945), *Maine—Nine Poems* (1981), *A Northern Calendar* (1982)

Charles Simic (b. 1938), *Classic Ballroom Dances* (1980), *Austerities* (1982)

Jim Simmerman (b. 1952), *Home* (1983), *Once Out of Nature* (1985)

Dave Smith (b. 1942), *Dream Flights* (1981), *In the House of the Judge* (1983)

William Stafford (b. 1914), *Smoke's Way* (1983), *Roving Across Fields* (1983)

George Starbuck (b. 1931), *Talkin' B.A. Blues* (1980), *The Argot Merchant Disaster* (1982)

Gerald Stern (b. 1925), *The Red Coal* (1981), *Paradise Poems* (1984)

Anne Stevenson (b. 1933), *The Fiction-Makers* (1985), *Selected Poems* (1985)

Mark Strand (b. 1934), *The Late Hour* (1978), *Selected Poems* (1980)

Richard Tillinghast (b. 1940), *Sewanee in Ruins* (1981), *Our Flag Was Still There* (1984)

Ellen Bryant Voigt (b. 1943), *Claiming Kin* (1976), *The Forces of Plenty* (1983)

David Wagoner (b. 1926), *Who Shall Be the Sun?* (1978), *In Broken Country* (1979)

Robert Penn Warren (b. 1905), *Chief Joseph of the Pence Nez* (1983), *Selected Poems, 1923 – 1985* (1985)

James Whitehead (b. 1936), *Domains* (1966), *Local Mew* (1979)

Richard Wilbur (b. 1921), *Walking to Sleep* (1969), *The Mind-Reader* (1976)

Nancy Willard (b. 1936), *A Visit to William Blake's Inn* (1981), *Household Tales of Moon and Water* (1982)

Miller Williams (b. 1930), *Distractions* (1981), *The Boys on Their Bony Mules* (1983)

Charles Wright (b. 1935), *Country Music: Selected Early Poems* (1982), *The Other Side of the River* (1984)

Paul Zimmer (b. 1934), *Earthbound Zimmer* (1983), *The American Zimmer* (1984)